Junkette

Sarah Shotland

ISBN: 0988445921
ISBN-13: 978-0-9884459-2-5

For BLP

Perhaps all pleasure is only relief
—*William S. Burroughs, Junky*

Not that it was beautiful,
but that, in the end, there was
a certain sense of order there;
something worth learning
in that narrow diary of my mind,
in the commonplaces of the asylum
where the cracked mirror
or my own selfish death
outstared me . . .
I tapped my own head;
it was glass, an inverted bowl.
It's a small thing
to rage inside your own bowl.
At first it was private.
Then it was more than myself.
Anne Sexton, More Than Myself

I

Louisiana heat isn't about temperature, it's about pressure—the weight of heavy air pushing against your temples. Pushes the rightness of judgment right out.

I've seen it happen. Otherwise rational, otherwise peaceable people just go ahead and lose their minds out of their heads. Fuck the air conditioning and fuck a cold shower. I never knew elbows could sweat until I moved here.

After last summer, number five, I said never again. Here it is September, and here I am again. Everybody's a stewed chicken. You could win the Powerball and still wind up without a brain cell working in this kind of pressure cooker.

Dan Rather's set up shop on the Riverwalk, talking about how Ivan is going to be the big-time storm. All my rich Tulane friends have evacuated to ranches in Texas.

Me and 100,000 other people, we're getting out of this city today.

But I'm not coming back.

It might not be this one, and it might not be the next one, but sooner or later, I will die in the water—boiled or suffocated or swimming or stewed, drowned in the bathtub.

It's not raining yet, which makes most folks think drowning is a long way off, but the old ladies who drink gin on their porches say you don't drown until the rain passes, once the water's rising, when you're trudging through it. They say when the water's coming from the wrong direction is when you have to worry. But what do they know? They're still alive.

∾

The chances of drowning in Boulder are slim. Trust me, I'm good at numbers. I'm good at research. Only 3 people died by drowning last year.

Other causes of death included:

43 suicides

1 "struck by a tree"

4 homicides (4 homicides!)

72 falls

2 acute ethanol inhalations

3 asphyxiations by food

I'm pretty sure I can manage not to get struck by a tree or fall myself to death.

∾

Now, death in New Orleans is a whole other animal:

98 drownings

189 suicides

0 "struck by tree"

274 homicides

91 falls
36 acute ethanol inhalations
112 asphyxiations by food

∽

They won't let anyone change the TV from the Weather Channel, which seems ridiculous. That's why we're here. Ivan the Terrible. Ivan the Beast. But Ivan is my ticket right out of this city.

I don't care about Mack. I don't care about the Moonlight. I will find another crappy boyfriend and another crappy job. In fact, I will find a glorious boyfriend and a glorious job.

I will read books all the way from New Orleans to Boulder, I've got a backpack full of them.

I have a ten-pack of foils tucked tight and sweaty between my tits, and that'll last me until I get there. At which point, I will do my last foil and breathe the mountain air and forget about drowning.

∽

"One to Boulder, Colorado."

"Return?" The woman behind the bulletproof glass doesn't look up from her computer. Her nails are so long they span the length of the keyboard. I wonder if they are an impediment to typing.

"Nope."

She looks up. "You sure? It's more expensive to get two one-ways."

"Positive," I say. I smile despite my best efforts to contain myself.

"Suit yourself," she says. "Don't say I didn't warn you."

I unfold fives and tens and ones until I get to seventy-eight. Slide the stack through the opening at the bottom of the window.

"And a pack of Kools," I say.

She glares.

"Just a joke. You know, cause of your window thing."

"All tickets sold today are refundable and transferrable for the next year."

"No extra charge?" I ask.

"No. Required by state laws, emergency evacuations." She prints my ticket. "Gate 7B, leaves in," she looks at the clock, "three hours, forty-two minutes. Next."

∽

With a $78 ticket, plus the $75 ten-pack of foils, I'll have $90 for Boulder until I find a job there. Even Mayor Nagin told people to leave with money, bring some Benjamins, he said. I didn't think I was going to spend so much on the foils, but once you buy five, you might as well buy ten. Chip knew I was leaving town and didn't want to see me go—none of my boys want to see me go—so he threw in a freebie to try and make sweet. It's best to leave places when people still want you to stay. Means you can always come back.

I probably need more money, though.

∞

From the National Atmospheric and Oceanic Administration:

The eye at a hurricane's center is a relatively calm, clear area approximately 20-40 miles across.

Do not focus on the eye—hurricanes are immense systems that can move in complex patterns that are difficult to predict. Be prepared for changes in size, intensity, speed and direction.

∞

Last night, I sucked Mack's dick for forty minutes. I know because we put the lasagna in the microwave, got naked, and when the timer went off, he still hadn't come.

Mack says it's not my fault, that junkies have trouble coming. Just one more thing we have trouble getting right.

∞

"Mama, I wanna cold drink."

I am not sure which one of the women nearby is this child's mother.

"Mama, I wanna cold drink."

The women nearby may have the same confusion, because none of them appear to register this request as a directive.

"Mama. Mama. Mama, I wanna cold drink. Thirsty. It's hot in here. Mama, can I have a cold drink?"

This could go on for hours.

∾

I go outside and sit on my backpack, light a cigarette and enjoy the breeze. There are fifteen days of tolerable weather in New Orleans—spring is quick here. It lasts for the first weekend of Jazz Fest and disappears before the second weekend begins. People make the mistake of coming for the second weekend to hear the big headliners, but they end up miserable. Fine with me, means they spend more money at the bars trying to stay cool.

It only takes a Category 4 to give us a nice breezy day.

∾

I am too smart to be a junky. I am too smart to be a bartender, but I am also too smart to take a research job that will pay me half the money for twice the hours. I am too smart to stay in this city. I am ready to make good on my IQ. This is the best decision I will ever make. Boulder, Colorado.

∾

The line for cold drinks is getting longer while the line for tickets is getting shorter. The TVs keep telling us hurricanes are unpredictable. The shorter line is still out the door, spills onto Loyola Avenue.

∾

Most people make the mistake of believing the movies they see about junkies. Most people think junkies are skinny, emaciated even. I only wish. I can't blame people. I thought the same thing. Which is one reason I am so bitter about this whole affair. I thought I might lose a few pounds at least.

∾

The chairs in the Greyhound Station are purple, green and gold. As if everything in the whole fucking city needs to be carnival themed. This city doesn't know shit about less is more. I am understated. I am subtle. That is something that junkies actually are—we are subtle people, subdued, quiet by and large. But not necessarily thin.

Take the woman sitting across from me on the purple chair. She looks like there's a bubble between her bones and her skin, pouches of air making her into a cloud. Most people would never think junky, but I know better. This lady's so far down into a bag of dope, I almost ask if I can buy a piece off her.

People never think about the fact that dope makes it so you can't move. Makes it so you stay in one place and even moving your eyelids seems like aerobics.

That kind of not moving makes a person fat.

Sometimes I think about all the shit that's stacking up inside my body. When I get to Boulder I'm going to do one of those all-natural colon cleanses.

∾

I try to read a little Ginsberg, from the Naked Poetry collection, but I can't get past the first couple of lines. Ginsberg used to be my favorite. Used to make me feel like I was really getting my junky on. Now I feel like I get it more than he got it, I'd rather hear about the beauty of stillness and snow and the leaves and the woods and all the stupid shit that bored me before. Now I want it.

∾

I know I will be better for having left, but looking at the stops on the bus route, none of those places is New Orleans. Laredo. Childress. Rocky Ford. Boulder's no slap the ground when the bass gets low kind of a place, no magnolia petals in the sunlight, no fatback goodness, bread sopping, hot and creamy kind of a place. No heavy with the weight of slave ghosts and their Gods. New Orleans may be Catholic, but it does a righteous job of putting aside guilt.

But I could use a little more guilt in my life, I could use a little more shame. There are some things worth feeling shame about.

∽

My ringing phone blinks CAUTION HASSAN. Hassan is my boss. He probably wants to know why I'm not at the Moonlight, why I'm not unsmudging glasses right now, why I'm not rearranging beer bottles into neat rows. God knows I could use the money.

Everybody knows you make the most money during Mardi Gras and hurricanes, and everybody knows you'd rather make the money from the locals who stay for a hurricane than tourists who come for carnival. The Moonlight won't close if the levees break. The Moonlight only closes for people shooting movies, and even then, it's because the movie people pay Hassan more to close than he'd make to stay open.

∽

Hassan says he'll pay me $50 to come in, to show up. There's another route to Boulder tomorrow, same time, although according to the TV, we might not be here tomorrow.

Everyone knows you can't move with less than $100. Why do I think I can outsmart the things everybody knows? I bet that kid in there still doesn't have her cold drink.

∽

II

The movie people like the Moonlight's old neon sign.

The movie people like its heavy door.

The movie people like the moulding and the courtyard and the marigolds you can see blooming in Sophie B. Wright Park.

Sophie B. Wright Park also allows for large crews to assemble, to count snakes of electrical cord and check down clipboards, to smoke cigarettes and spray paint props in the open air.

Sophie B. Wright Park is barely a park at all, though. More like a quadruple-wide neutral ground with some magnolia trees and a couple benches, the statue of Miss Sophie B. Wright. It's for the ladies who try to make a few bucks once the sun goes down. Today, though, there are people out, walking their dogs. The people who know better than to get ruffled about a nice breezy day—got the day off, take a nice walk with the dog.

∾

Mumps drops me off outside the Moonlight.

"Thanks for the ride, Mumps."

"I'm glad you didn't jump ship, Claire."

"Eh. We'll see. Just postponed."

"Well, the longer you postpone, the longer I get to see you. Let me know if you want a ride when you get off. Grace is at a work thing all week."

Grace is Mumps' girlfriend. Grace doesn't like me. Mumps does, though.

"Hey, Claire."

"Hey, what?"

"You got a spare you can float me? Get you back when you get off work. I'm going to Chip's later."

I take one of the foil envelopes out of my bra, put it in the cup holder.

"Don't worry about getting me back. Thanks for the ride."

❧

Hassan is behind the bar, which is never good.

"Cah-lay," he calls in his singsongy, lady register as I walk in the door, "Cah-lay." Hassan has never learned to hit the end of English words even though he has lived in the States for fifteen years and married a fat blonde from New Iberia. Claire is Cah-lay, and Michael is Mi-kah, and Stephanie is Stefan. He has trouble with ys and rs, and ings are totally out of the question, which isn't an issue as most people around here don't have a firm grasp on the pronunciation of anything continuous.

"Cah-lay, I'm so happ to see you."

He scuttles to the end of the bar and hands me a tumbler with ice and what smells like butterscotch liqueur.

"Hassan, what are you making?" I smile pretty, almost wink.

"The lady at the end wants a butter-nipp," he says.

"Good thing I'm here," I say. "You can leave that fifty in the cash box with the bank."

"You make lots of the money tonight, Cah-lay, all the cops say the storm is change."

"I saw on the TV."

"You be a good girl, Cah-lay, you call if you run out of toilet pape."

Hassan leaves the paper supply closet locked at all times because he thinks the guys in the kitchen steal the toilet paper. He's probably right.

∽

The cops who hang out at the Moonlight are okay for the most part. Dumas, who's here most often, isn't half-bad. At first, it was off-putting to have cops staring at me from the corners all night long, but now I understand why Hassan wants them here.

The cash box isn't bolted down to the back counter. People act drunk and wander behind the bar. I've seen people jump the bar for a reach and grab, after a long night of video poker.

But the cooks can walk behind the bar, too—get a cup of Coke or use the phone. I've walked out a couple nights with nothing because my drawer's been exactly a hundred dollars short. It isn't that hard to quick slip a bill in a pocket.

∽

The guys in the back aren't happy. This is the age-old conflict between front-of-the-house and back-of-the-house. Back makes just as much money no matter how busy things get, but front needs people. We've got people.

Everything else on Magazine St. is closed—Ms. Mae's and The Monkey Lounge and the Balcony Bar and the Bulldog. Juan's Flying Burrito is closed and I think St. Joe's is closed. Hassan has a knack for making money.

I can hear Mack bitching every time I send an order in. I don't know if Mack knew I was at the bus station, but I'd bet he's talked to Chip, and Chip would definitely tell him. Chip likes to be the carrier of all neighborhood gossip. He's a hen like that.

～

It's the kind of night when no one's ordering a pitcher of beer.

Everyone thinks they're original, ordering a hurricane. It isn't even funny, just a bitch to make. It's nine flippin' ingredients. It's even worse than a Long Island, because at least with a Long Island you just add Coke until it looks like the right shade of piss.

The bar's stacked two deep all the way down, and I turn the jukebox down and project. "Who's ordering a hurricane?" There's no response, like all of a sudden, nobody's drinking what they've been drinking all night long. "Who's ordering a hurricane? Raise your hand."

I see a couple hands go up in the back row, and once people see those hands, a few more go up, until it's just three people who have their hands at their sides, looking petrified of me.

I point at the first guy with his hands down, he's wearing a green Casey Jones cap.

"Good for you," I say. "It's your lucky night. Whatever you're drinking, as long as it only has two ingredients, on the house."

"I just want a High Life," he says.

"Even better." He gets his bubbly beer.

"What about you, lady?" It's one of our girls from Sophie B. Wright Park. I can guarantee she wants a shot of gin with olives and cherries.

"Shot of gin with olives and cherries," she says.

I grab a handful of green olives and maraschinos and throw them on a napkin, pour her a plastic go-cup half-full of McCormick's.

"Feel free to tip," I say.

"What about you, buddy?" The last guy with his arms down still looks a little shell-shocked even though if he'd been paying attention he'd know he's about to get a free drink.

"Can you make a margarita?" he asks.

"You're just as bad as the rest of them," I say.

❧

The regulars came in early, but they've been pushed out by all the hurricane drinkers. I miss the predictable shots of Rumpleminze and Goldschlager, the endless Jagers and Cuba Libres. I miss the whiskey sodas and gin and tonics and beer-beer-beer-beer-beer. We've suspended our usual nightly special of $1 anythings for the occasion of Ivan. We're the only place open, who needs a special.

∾

The rest of the night goes just like this, in big, plastic pitchers:

> Vodka
> Gin
> Light Rum
> Bacardi 151
> Triple Sec
> Amaretto
> Pineapple Juice
> Grapefruit Juice
> Grenadine

Most people think grenadine is cherry juice, but it's actually pomegranate.

∾

No one stops talking about Ivan even though we've had enough of the Weather Channel and everybody knows we won't see a drop of rain.

∾

The Moonlight kitchen closes at 3 A.M. If you order food after 2:30 something unfortunate may happen. Some things that aren't outside the realm of possibility:

Hamburger patty soccer
Lettuce dishrags
Olive earplugs
Spinach dip spiked with a little dish soap

One time I saw Benji rinse his used syringe out in a bowl of soup, which I thought was wholly inappropriate.

At 2:43, Mack comes out of the kitchen for the first time all night.

"So you decided to come to work after all, huh?"

"I need the money."

"You weren't going to say anything?"

"I didn't know what to say."

"Are you coming home after you get off?" He reaches for a go-cup.

"Where else am I going to go?" I ask. "What do you need?"

"Soda water with lime. You could go wherever it was you were heading."

"My plans changed," I say. I smile and hand him a soda water. "You want some whiskey with that water?"

"Probably should," he says, and I pour.

∾

At 4, Hassan calls and asks how business is going.

"We've slowed down now, but it was packed all night."

"You make the money, Cah-lay?"

"Yes, Hassan, I made the money."

"Good girl, that's my good Cah-lay. How are the nap-kis?"

"We're fine. Is anyone coming in for the morning shift?"

"I don't think so, Cah-lay. You go ahay and lock up at five."

"There's no one here now, Hassan. I'm gonna break down the bar."

"You lie to me, Cah-lay? Not just one perso?"

"Not even one, Hassan. I'd never lie to you. You're spending money keeping the lights on."

"You smart girl, Cah-lay. See you the weekend."

III

When I get to the Josephine Street Boarding House, I see our TV blinking through the upstairs window, and I hear the phone in Warring's room downstairs. It rings and rings, and then someone picks it up. Warring lives in the only room with a phone. Since he has cancer, he'll need to call an ambulance and pays $5 extra a week for it.

Warring is the only person we know in the building— maybe he's the only one who's stuck around for us to get to know. The last guy I saw moving in and right back out was a firefighter. Or at least he was wearing a Fire Department t-shirt, and his arms looked like what I imagine a brave man's arms are supposed to look like.

❧

I stay on the porch for a few minutes on the rocking chairs. Mack's watching the morning news—all Mack ever watches is the news, but the morning broadcast is the worst. I'd rather sit out here and feel the day get light.

❧

From the outside, the Josephine place looks respectable, like a bed and breakfast even, with one of those big, Southern porches painted fresh white and three oversized rocking chairs. There are plants, I don't know who waters them.

I've never met our landlord. Mack's been living here for a couple years, I just moved in a couple months ago, so Mack still takes care of the rent. $100 per week, per person. We don't tell the landlord I moved in. The downside is we only have one key.

Inside, there's definitely not fresh paint. The banister is sticky and dusty at the same time, sometimes I think I can see dust stuck in the sticky, like the box of porn Mack keeps in the box underneath his bed.

Someone's struggling to open the heavy front door with the triple locks, and I regret having lingered on the porch.

But it's just Jennifer, and she's the only person walking onto the porch who could possibly make me take back my regret. Jennifer stays with Warring—she's like the human version of the emergency phone, only she doesn't cost $5 a week extra. She costs Oxycotins off the top of every prescription. Which Warring doesn't mind.

"Good morning, Miss," Jennifer smiles underneath her hair. It's so long it looks like she gets extensions, but it's real—black with wide chunks of platinum streaked in the front. It doesn't look trashy on her.

I've never dyed my hair. Chemicals that close to the skull seem like a bad idea.

"Morning."

"You're up so early."

"You're up so early," I say right back to her.

"I have the early shift."

"And I had the late one," I say.

"You guys gonna be around later?" she asks, and I nod, because I'm pretty sure Mack has the night off, and I'm not on the schedule again until the weekend. "Good, I'm gonna come knock on your door. I need some human contact," she says.

"We'll be here, I'm sure. Or at Chip's."

"It just gets so depressing down there, sometimes, with all the other girls and Warring sick and," she trails off for a minute, puts her big pink sunglasses on and looks into what has suddenly become a bright morning. "You know the drill," she says. She unchains her bike from the side of the house—a big, green cruiser with a basket on the front, and a bell, which she likes to ring for effect when she arrives and departs.

She straddles the seat and turns back for a second, "Y'all be good," she says, like being good could mean anything at all.

∾

When I get upstairs, Mack is sprawled on the bed in his boxers, an empty tub of onion dip on the floor.

"They've been yapping all night," he says.

Jennifer's not the only one who stays with Warring, although she's the only tolerable one. The rest of them are prostitutes, but not streetwalkers, just middle-aged ladies who go on dates they get paid for. They aren't call girls either. Their dates aren't with businessmen who use some kind of discreet service. They're just middle-aged ladies who happen to know some lonely middle-aged men who will pay them to fuck.

Sometimes they have apartments, and sometimes they'll rent a room at Josephine Street for a week or two, but usually they just crash on Warring's floor and pretend to be nurses.

They make a lot of noise. I don't see how Warring can sleep. But Warring sleeps through anything. All those Oxys.

"I swear, they never get tired of talking," Mack says, and flips off the TV. "News is on loop," he says. "How was work? You make some money?"

"Thank god," I nod. "All those fucking hurricanes."

The foils are still tucked between my tits, and I don't want to share, but I'm back at home and I should do something to make Mack forget about the almost leaving part of my day, so I shake them out of my shirt and onto the floor by the onion dip.

Mack likes the way I look on my hands and knees, so I stay down there for a couple seconds, let my back arch a little while I gather the foils and look up at him, smile.

"So you were stocking up for your trip, huh?"

"You wanna get right?" I ask.

"Of course, baby."

Mack loves to call me baby.

❧

This is who lives in 70130:
> Me and Mack and Chip and Benji, Jennifer and Warring and Ra and Vern and Erica
> A bunch of other people I don't know, and some I sort of know
> 21 registered sex offenders

8,011 black people
4,380 white people
1,500 Asian people
Approximately 1,000 people who refuse to report racial demographics in the census

∾

For the first time, I have the upper hand, and Mack knows it.

I can feel it in the way he's looking while I cook the dope, and I feel it in the way he avoids raising his voice or talking about the bus ticket I've got tucked in my purse.

I go ahead and do my shot first.

It feels a little like all those other first times you realize you're different, that you've got the power.

∾

The first time I shot heroin, I didn't know I was high at all. It was like the first time I tripped LSD. I didn't know if what I was feeling was what I was supposed to be feeling, if the chemical had any bearing on the feeling at all.

It was with a dude whose name I don't remember.

He was at Ms. Mae's, which used to be called The Club, and now the sign says both "Ms. Mae's" and "The Club," so people call it whatever happens to fall out of their mouth.

I call it Ms. Mae's because I like alliteration.

I was there with my boyfriend before Mack. That would be Jimmy. Jimmy didn't read—not that he didn't know how, just that he chose not to. I always thought it was strange he wanted to date me, but his willingness was enough. Jimmy had dropped out of Tulane when we met, and he thought I was cute. I was still in school. I was younger than most people there anyway because I left high school three semesters early and went straight to Tulane. I'm good at tests.

Jimmy didn't believe in monogamy, and I was young enough or stupid enough that I didn't believe in monogamy either. Until he fucked someone else first. I thought we were just saying it—saying it the same way we said we didn't believe in war or eating meat or wearing tight pants. If there were to be a question of monogamy, I figured I'd get laid before he did.

Jimmy was kind of funny looking—real tall and lanky with a long, long torso and a tribal tattoo around his belly button. One time, someone asked him what his tattoo meant and he said, "It means I'm fucking sexy."

Jimmy was flirting with some girl at Ms. Mae's, and so I started flirting with the one guy who didn't seem to be hitting on anyone else. When he asked me if I did dope, I thought he was talking about pot. So we went to his apartment.

When the guy showed me the needle, I wasn't scared at all. I put my arm out. He asked me what kind of music I wanted to listen to—he had at least ten of those giant CD books stacked next to a really nice stereo system in the crappiest apartment I'd ever seen.

I said Tribe Called Quest. It seemed like the sort of thing to request, even though I couldn't even name a song from Tribe Called Quest. He put it on the stereo and we fucked on an air mattress and he told me not to be like him, to never become like him, and that he needed to get some more dope, that we should go to the Moonlight, you could always get dope there.

Now I know that was the first night I ever saw Mack, or Benji, or Chip. Only I didn't know their names, and I didn't care about who they were, and I was only thinking about how wonderful it was that I could speak my mind, that everything seemed absolutely fine to say. That I could say anything I fucking wanted.

I went home and told Jimmy exactly what happened, a complete blow by blow. Before then, I'd never even told him I hated shrimp. He used to cook shrimp for me all the time.

∾

I feel the same way I felt after kissing a girl for the first time. You walk through the grocery store and wonder if everyone can tell, if you suddenly look like the kind of person who kisses girls. If you suddenly look like the kind of person who shoots up. If you suddenly look like the kind of person who owns all her power or knows what dope means.

∾

"I'm still going to leave," I say, after we've gotten right. We're lying on the bed, scratching each other's backs.

"I want to go too, baby. I really, really do. I just want to get some money together first."

"Me too," I say.

"That's why I think we should move in with Chip."

"I think that's the worst idea I've ever heard," I say. I still like dope for making me say whatever I'm thinking.

"Why?"

"Because there's a million fucking people in and out of that house all day long."

"But that's just because Chip likes company," Mack says, like he's not as smart as he is, like I'm suddenly going to forget that he's the smartest man I've ever dated.

"Chip doesn't like the company," I say, "Chip likes to sell dope."

"We'd save a lot of money that way, baby. He only pays three hundred bucks a month for that place."

"That's because it's a shit hole."

"It has a kitchen, at least. I want to be able to cook for you."

"I don't think we should move in with Chip."

"Well, how are we going to save money, then? How are we going to be able to get out of here if we don't save money? If we move in, Chip's gonna give us dope cheaper—you know he is. You know how much he likes you, baby."

"And then we'd save that money, too, I guess." That point I'm willing to concede.

"Exactly, baby. I'm telling you, Claire, I want us to get out of here, together. Do stuff, write, read, travel. I want to see things with you, baby. You're the only woman I've ever met who gets it the way you get it."

He starts stroking the hairs on my neck, giving me little kisses on the back of my ears. He starts thinking he's winning me over, but I'm still the one with the ticket in my purse.

"Plus, we've got to stay here at least for a couple more months, at least until after the election. We've got to vote."

"Who gives a shit about voting?"

"Claire. We've been over this. We live in a democracy. As citizens, it's our duty to engage in civil discourse, in asserting our voices. No one else is going to represent us except us."

"I understand what the word democracy means."

"I thought you were excited about voting. I thought you were looking forward to that." He kisses me soft again in the hollow of my collarbone. "Since you've never done it before. Since it'll be your first time."

He can keep on talking. Voting isn't gonna be power like this.

∾

I wake up in the middle of the afternoon sunlight and sneak out of the house like a whisper before Mack can feel me gone.

∾

The only person besides Mack who cares that I'm still here is Chico, so I go to the Marigny and make an appearance.

Chico isn't at his apartment on Royal, so I go to St. Claude where he keeps his babies. Rows and rows of lights and dirt and bright green. Chico rejects all things hydroponic. Plants grow in dirt, he says. It's just the dummies who don't use dirt.

"So you didn't get on the rattle bus, huh? You're a coward," Chico says when he sees me.

"I'm not a coward. I'm just broke," I say.

"And you tell me, little skinny girl, why you so broke?"

"Because people don't tip for shit."

"You're a liar," he says, and keeps pruning his babies.

"You didn't leave either. That make you a coward?"

"Can't leave the babies." He snips a crinkled leaf from the bottom of a bud pod.

"So you wouldn't leave those babies if it meant you might drown, Chico?"

"I live on the high ground part of the city, stupid. I stay with my babies. I leave my babies, someone else stay to steal them. People in the dry part stay to keep watch." God, he can be so melodramatic, especially with that accent.

"I came down because I thought you'd be happy to see me," I say.

"I'll be happy when you leave."

"Thanks."

"You think Chico can't survive without some skinny-ass gringo girl?" he says. "You'll learn." I can feel a lecture coming on. Chico has plenty to say about most things. "You know the people in New York think I'm dead?"

"Yes, I know, Chico."

"But you really think they think I'm dead for real? Some of the time you have to die to a place. You don't die to the people."

"I'm not faking my own death, Chico."

"I'm not faking either, Chica. That place is my bodies. You want bodies? You can't even get on a rattle bus, you're so scared. Let's see how scared you are with bodies on the top of you. You think you're real cool, don't you? You think you're real cool with that fat boy—the baldy one. I see him around. I don't like that fat, baldy boy. And he's not so cool, and you're not so cool. You're just scaredy kitten."

"It's scaredy cat."

He points his pruning shears in my direction. "You just a little kitten, though. Skinny kitten, too. You can't be with bodies on you."

"I don't have bodies on me, Chico."

"You gonna get them. You think I have to die to a place with no regrets? That's the only reason you have to die to a place. Why you think I spend all my time with my babies now? These babies don't stack bodies. But all that dopey business, that's the bodies—everything costs you something with that dopey stuff. What do you say, with the coin counting?"

"The coin counting?"

"You know, you give me a nickel, you give me a dime, for every stupid little nonsense thing."

"I think you're thinking nickeled and dimed. We say, like, the bank is nickel and diming me to death."

"Yeah, yeah, but not the bank. The dope."

"You charge people for the weed, Chico."

"But not charging for the cab ride to take it to the house, not charging for the baggie, not charging for the lights and dirt, stupid girl. Not charging to share a joint." The t's on Chico's nots are barely there, they drift up to the sky like smoke.

"Those things are built in to your price structure, Chico. You're not losing money on this shit, you've got bills to pay."

"You want to argue."

∾

Chico is right, I do want to argue, and as soon as I walk into the apartment, Mack starts about how filthy the place is and I can't help it, I pop. Mack says something about leaving if I want to leave and how much nicer his life would be without me, always having to teach me which way is up and that I really am just some college kid trying to slum it for a little while before I go West for my next clichéd shitty adventure, and I want to tell him things. I want to tell him there are a lot of ways to slum it, and I didn't have to choose him. About how clichés are ubiquitous around here, every junky is a fucking cliché, but when I say ubiquitous, Mack says I'm pretentious, and when he says it, it's just proof you can be smart without school, so I keep not saying it. I keep not saying anything and Mack pushes me out the door and says through the deadbolt, leave.

Mack doesn't say anything when he opens the door, he just pushes it open and lets it hang there.

I V

I'm locked inside the apartment, but Mack will be back soon. He should have been back forty-five minutes ago, Chip's place is only a block and a half away. But he probably wants to make me wait. We had been getting along so well, then I ruined it all again. I really don't give a shit about all that, though.

I'm more worried about myself than my missing boyfriend. I can't find my ticket. I knew I shouldn't have taken it out of my purse.

Soon as I find my ticket, he'll get his lesson.

He wants the apartment clean? He wants to bitch at me for the state of the fucking apartment? Like I'm all of a sudden Suzy Homemaker, tidy up the nursery? I didn't realize he required pristine conditions to watch the debates. It's fucking clean, now. But I didn't clean for him. I had to find my ticket, so I threw shit in a garbage bag. Let him make me wait. Gives me more time to find the fucking thing.

The only place I've taken it out of my purse was this room. Mack says apartment, like we've got a kitchen or closets or doorways, but it's a room.

At least we have a bathroom.

☙

Retrace my steps. Retrace my steps. Fucking losing everything all the time. So I was looking for that foil, turned my purse inside out. By the time I'd found it, I really needed to use it, then I forgot to put my purse back together. I'm so fucking stupid. That ticket's got to be in here somewhere.

☙

I admit that Mack had me sold on the election shit, so I'll send Louisiana an absentee. I'll vote early. Whatever. I'm leaving as soon as I find that ticket. I need to get to Boulder.

☙

Let's see how clean this place is without me. Let him watch the debates without me. See how fun it'll be to talk politics when I'm not there to absorb the bitching. When he gets home he'll give me those little kisses, all soft at the collarbone. He'll bring me back an extra foil, try to make it better with dope. But I'll still be gone tomorrow.

☙

I don't know why there's always trash on the floor. It's not like we own stuff. When we get back from work, we let cigarette boxes and belts and panties fall to the floor, and by the time we wake up in the afternoon, we've gotta be at work, so we sniff out the best of the floor and run off to clock in.

∾

I shoved all the Styrofoam containers of half-eaten leftovers to the bottom, mealybugs crawling out of hamburgers and crawfish.

It all went in:

> Stray playing cards, crinkly and rough from drying after we spilled beer on them
> 30 empty cigarette boxes
> Abitas, Anchor Steams, Woodchucks, High Lifes
> Soup cans
> Last strands of Twizzler Pull 'N Peels (neither of us like that last single strand)
> All those half-aluminum cans, shivved and burnt-bottomed

∾

The way Mack likes to cook the dope is strange. I don't understand why he doesn't like to use spoons. Says it's bad luck, something about the one time he used a spoon, he got busted, so this place looks like a recycling dump, all those stupid cans.

∾

Here's something I've always wished for: a complete consumptive inventory upon death. I want to see the accumulation of my own intake. A landfill overflowing with corncobs and wishbones and tea bags. A lake of wine and a ditch of

Ding-Dongs. I want to see the contrast of dopey foil and cokey plastic corners, see if the math works, if I have, in the end, gotten the perfect speedball balance.

This is what I think about when I clean. This is why I don't mind cleaning. I mind being told to clean.

❧

I imagine deep gorges of grits and Boulder. We don't talk about Boulder. Since I left the Greyhound Station last month with the exchange ticket, we've only discussed it twice—the night he told me he'd come, and during an argument about money. As soon as I muster up tears and whimper, but I love you, he takes me into his arms and holds me close to his belly and we get right and forgive each other. Boulder will be full of people I could love.

❧

So the trash is gone, but there's a giant pile of crinkled foil wrappers by the bed. I don't know why we keep them, Mack always tells me to lick them clean even though I hate the way dope tastes on my tongue. Just like it on the inside, that's why I bang—to avoid the bitter tongue. I guess we keep them in case of an emergency. Sometimes I want to make a giant ball of tinfoil, lay on my back and throw it up, let it bounce off my stomach.

❧

I wish I could go for a walk, get my plan straight, but he took the key. The debate starts in twenty minutes and I know he doesn't want to miss it. Mack watches presidential debates the way some men watch the Super Bowl. He needs the pre-game commentary and the post-game analysis. The commercials aren't as entertaining, but that gives us time to bitch.

Mack'll be happy that I cleaned up for this, did something to make it look like a girl lives here. It's not like I can cook, with our no stove, so we eat a lot of candy. I like to see Mack happy, I like that smile, I love those little make-up kisses. Maybe Mack really will come to Boulder with me, maybe we can both get clean. We could both start hiking, eat vitamins.

Mack won't let the moving in with Chip thing go. He's got an extra room, but I don't see the sense in it. Mack talks like he's in rush-hour traffic going back and forth, when it's a block and a half. There's an alley that connects Josephine Street to Felicity Street. That's what he means when he says we're not being efficient.

As if we moved into Chip's place we'd be waiting any less.

We wait for Ra to make his deliveries and then we wait for Chip to weigh and bundle. If we moved into Chip's place we'd spend our whole lives waiting. We'd always be there when Ra left, so we'd always be waiting for him to get back.

∾

I gather the foils in my arms, bring them onto the bed. The lamp isn't doing much, not more than the glow of the TV, so I switch the plugs. Lamp off. Box on. The debate logo splashes across the screen, an ugly cartoon eagle, an uglier wave of a red, white and blue flag. I should have gone into marketing, advertising. I'd be at the top of my field. I've got an eye for things. I know what ugly looks like. Instead, I'm a fucking bartender. Waste of my eye, though there's plenty ugly that crosses that bar, too. That's for fucking sure. It's a skill helpful in any profession, really. Maybe that's what I'll do when I get to Boulder. Marketing or editing, maybe I could design book jackets.

∾

As the commercials roll in, I smooth each foil and stack them neat, one on top of the other, and start counting. At seventy-nine, the stack topples, and I start over, making squatter buildings of foil. They're thinner than pennies. All glued together, they wouldn't take up the space of a dollar, but I think how many dollars they're worth. My god, we make a lot of money.

At 148, I stop. I'm worried. Mack still isn't home. I wish I could keep minutes on my phone, wish Mack had a phone, wish we had a house phone, wish someone had a fucking phone. Phone booths are stationary and we are moving. It was a smart person who came up with the cell phone.

There's nothing to do with these foils. They are cleaned and organized. The floor is bare except for dust too small to clean without a broom. The clothes are folded and tucked away in the corner beside the radiator. Mack's books are in alphabetical order. The porn videos are in a neat pyramid, mixtapes in a tower. There's nothing left to do but the last full foil we've got, but I'm not in the mood to keep fighting tonight.

∾

Everything tidy and placed and still no ticket.

∾

The Super Bowl has better ads, but there are still beer commercials. Taste the Rockies. I will taste the fucking Rockies, but I won't drink shitty-ass Coors, I'll drink heady microbrews and refill my growlers. Everyone in Colorado drinks good beer, there's nice pot. Denver is the only place in the United States with traceable amounts of marijuana in the air. I'd love to live in a state like that. I wonder if New Orleans has traceable amounts of piss in the air. If that's our claim to fame.

I look for my ticket under the bed, between the bed and the wall, under the mattress, maybe I thought I was hiding it someplace I'd never forget. I look under the radiator and double-check all my pockets. I look in the mini-fridge and the microwave and shake out all the books.

There's nothing to do but empty the trash and start over. I heave the garbage bag to the floor and start with the paper trash, the after-show flyers and the takeout menus. I grab fistfuls of envelopes and guest checks. The last drippings from the soup cans and beer bottles have made everything wet. Like this fucking city.

∾

It makes more sense to vote in Colorado. Living in the South, my vote doesn't even count. In Colorado, I've got a shot at counting.

∾

The floor is covered in trash, Mack's gonna be pissed, I'm sticky and the debates are starting. If Mack doesn't come back soon, I'm doing that last foil. Or maybe I should save it, what if he doesn't come back. What if he's been picked up? What if I have to stay here indefinitely? Mack will come back. Mack will be back soon. The only thing left is the leftovers. It wouldn't be in there.

∾

The door unlocks. Mack. Shit.

"What the fuck are you doing?"

"What does it look like I'm doing? I'm going through the fucking trash. I'm looking for something."

"What did you do with my onion dip?"

"It was bad."

"I bought that yesterday, I could have eaten that."

"Where have you been?"

"I was at Chip's. I got you something, beautiful." He leans over me, over the trash, there's those kisses. "I got us a kick-down, baby. I talked to Ra for a while, too. What did you say to him the last time you saw him? Cause he really likes you. You should think about that, you know it wouldn't be that bad if you and he—"

"Nothing, I don't know what I said to him, probably nothing."

Mack's annoying me. He's acting like we didn't get into a huge fight, like he didn't storm out of the house and then make me wait forever to get right.

"Has the debate started?" The trumpets are back and I can hear the dumb swoosh sound that goes along with the ugly eagle. Mack steps over me and all the trash, lies on the bed, turns up the TV. "Come on, what could you be looking for? Come get right."

"I don't want a fucking get-right. I'm busy."

I take that back. Of course I want to get right.

"Where's that can?"

"Just use a spoon like a normal person," I snap.

"Those are for my soup."

"Get over it, the cans are trashed. You're the one who wanted the apartment clean. We can take some new spoons from work tomorrow."

Mack shakes his head and sighs, picks one of the sliced cans from the mess of trash and takes it to the bathroom, I can hear the faucet running and the flicker of fire. "Get in here, Claire. Come on, baby, this'll make you feel better. It's good this time."

I let him feel like he's making me feel better. Now I don't feel so pissed. I let him do it for me, let him softly whisper things while he looks for the red register, and then it comes like it always does, and it's nothing special.

∿

We go back to the bed, and Kerry criticizes our involvement in the Middle East and Baby Bush shakes his head and pretends to be writing a note to himself, like he can write. He's probably drawing little pictures of cows and airplanes and clouds with mean faces.

"Neither of them are any different, listen to this joker," Mack says over Kerry, "this is a fucking pox upon the republic, this is a fucking joke, a joke, a really bad joke."

∿

I leave the bed and start sorting through the trash again. The first box smells like fish, fuck. Another reason I hate this city, if it doesn't smell like piss, it smells like fish. I don't even eat fish, Mack bringing all these nasty-ass bottom feeder swamp bugs into our place. I open it up, turn my head, there's about two-hundred tiny black bugs, little tiny baby roaches they look like, crawling around the crawfish heads.

"Baby! What the fuck are you looking for?"

"I'm just looking for something." I don't want to tell him I'm looking for the ticket, and I don't feel like telling him I love him.

Jim Lehrer thanks the University of Miami before the cut to commercial and Mack leaves the bed and rubs my shoulders. I shove the top back down on the roaches and skeletons and take the next box out. It's mostly empty, a giant piece of lettuce, no bugs. Then a box with soggy French fries and a mound of dried-up ketchup and hot sauce.

"Baby, stop."

"I have to find my fucking ticket. I could trade that for sixty bucks. That's all I have left to trade."

"Why do you need to trade anything, Claire? You've got a job, we're fine, baby, we're doing good. You don't need that ticket."

"Where's my fucking ticket?"

∾

There are two more boxes left. The first one has the tiny roaches on the outside of it. I shove it away from me and get the next one, which is lighter, but smells worse. There's a baby roach on my wrist, I flick it off, it lands on Mack's leg and he shakes.

"You've got to stop this. This is crazy, Claire."

I open the lighter box and it's just chicken bones and a little gristle, an empty container of blue cheese dressing and a shriveled piece of celery.

Mack grabs my hand, "Come on, stop."

I pull away from him and go to open the last box, he's right, this is crazy, my bus ticket isn't in a box of roach-infested takeout. I need to get to the mountains, I need some clean air, I need to get my fucking head right. I open the box, and there's the better part of a crawfish po-boy and a full order of macaroni and cheese, and there, right fucking there, there's my ticket.

I snatch my ticket and go to the bathroom, run the water and splash it over my face, tuck the ticket into my bra. I'm never taking this ticket out again.

I look at myself in the mirror. I may be crazy, but I was right.

❧

"Why was my ticket in that box?"

"You're asking me?"

"Fucking crawfish."

"Come here, Claire."

I take the ticket out of my bra and shove all my shit back into my purse, fold the ticket and hide it in the inside pocket. Zip, zip. I am exhausted. I lie down. Face the wall. Mack tries to wrap his arm around me, pull me to him, I flick him away. I get as close to the wall as I possibly can, touch it, feel its spackle on the tips of my fingers.

"Give me my foils." It's the only thing I can think to demand that I can get. I hear him stumbling around, pretending like he has to remember where he put them. "Give me my foils, they're mine." I turn away from the wall. Fucking TV. Why is this man President? Every junky I know is smarter than the motherfucking president. "Give me my foils."

"Give me a minute."

"If you wanted 'em, it wouldn't take a minute." I feel my face snarling.

"What are you so upset about? You want me to cook one for you? I could use another one, too. That's a good idea, let's cook another foil."

He holds them in the palm of his hand, I can see him counting them in his head, one, two, three, four, five, six. He wasn't lying about the kick-down, we got two extra. He could've just kept the two kicked down—he told me about them, though. We're a team. And here I am, lying to him, not even telling him I'm planning to leave, not being straight-up, not being real about what the fuck it is I'm looking for and why.

"I'm upset that my ticket was in that box, and yes, I do want you to cook one for me, I want you to cook two for me. Why was my ticket in the box with your food?"

Mack goes back to the bathroom. Kerry talks about how Bush never established an international coalition to fight in Iraq and Bush interrupts, which is against the rules, even I know that, and Bush says something dumb about Poland, Kerry forgot Poland.

Mack comes back to the bed with our full rigs and pulls me close to him.

"I want to know why my ticket was in there with that nasty crawfish that I don't fucking eat. You put that in there, didn't you?"

"Wait a second, baby, I want to hear this."

Kerry says something boring and pasty. Mack pulls my arm towards him. "Pump, baby, pump your fist for me."

I pump my fist and say it again, "I don't understand why it was in that fucking box."

I wait for him to press the steel into my skin and he looks at me and smiles and says, "I love you, Claire. I love you, baby."

"No."

"Just let me get my shit together so I can go with you. I love Colorado. I ever tell you about the time I jumped the Western Shortline? Beautiful shit. Right through the mountains. But I can't just leave right this minute."

I lie. "I'm not going right this minute."

Or maybe it's not a lie. I'm exhausted. I need money. Maybe I'll work for a week. Or maybe I should vote here and be in Colorado for the winter. I'll buy an advent calendar. When I get to Boulder, we'll open each cardboard door and take turns eating the stale chocolate, looking out at the white. I love those chocolate advent calendars. The anticipation.

"Then what's the problem, baby? Just let me get some shit together and we'll leave both of us. Listen." He turns my face to him, brushes my cheek like I'm made of china, "I love you, okay? You hear that? Come here." I nestle my head in his belly, he smells like olives. "You hear that?"

"I hear you."

"You know that?"

"I know that."

❧

V

Sometimes it's easier not to talk, even when I know Mack wants me to say something. Anything, no matter what it is, just to fill the space between our backs. But there's so much I don't know how to say, because I don't know what exactly it is that splits open inside me then sews itself back up, tight like a walnut.

The little pit inside me—it's made of something, and that something isn't anything like emptiness. It's got weight and mass and body.

∾

I had friends at Tulane. After blowing lines and buying bags of coke from the black guys who worked Oak Street, we'd be on our couches the next afternoon with headaches and grease stains on our fingers and they'd start in with the regret. It just feels like there's something empty inside me that I need to fill.

Then they'd get their parents to send them to the Ochsner Clinic, get all cleaned up and talk about a higher power.

I don't think I've ever felt empty inside. Most of the time, I'm full enough to vomit.

I know it would be better if I'd just say something to Mack, but I can't make myself.

I'd rather fill the space between our backs with thinking and maybe one night he'll finally understand that there's nothing I can say to make him believe anything is better than what's right here.

∾

Things with Pits:
    Peaches
    Arms
    Snakes

∾

We had a pecan tree in our backyard when I was a little girl. When the nuts fell, my mother would make my sister and I collect all the dirty pecans in our Easter baskets. Then she'd wash them and ask us what we wanted with pecans—cookies or brownies or blondie bars. My sister always wanted blondies and I always wanted brownies, and when she was in a good mood, my mother would make both and let us lick the mixing bowl and the beaters. But mostly she made us compromise. Then we'd pack the leftover pecans up in big gallon Ziplocs and stash them in the freezer.

We had pecans with everything—pesto made from pecans because my mother thought pine nuts were lavishly expensive. Spinach salads with candied pecans and strawberries. Pecan vinaigrette and pecan pie and pecan crusted chicken.

I hate pecans. No matter how much we washed them, they always tasted like dirt. Whenever I got my way and we made brownies, I'd suck all the chocolate off the nuts and leave a pile of broken pecans on my napkin.

Ungrateful, my mother would say, you know those cost money at the store.

∿

"Look what the cat dragged in today," Chip says a little too loudly as Mack throws our trash bags on the ground. No matter who it is or what time of day or night, Chip always says, look what the cat dragged in today. I don't think he realizes it implies that we look like wounded birds or bloodied rats or little piles of leaves.

"Bring that stuff in here and why don't we have a homecoming get-right," Chip says as he heaves the bags into 1464 Felicity Street, where the three of us live together as of now.

∿

There are a lot of ways to talk dope, but I think Chip talks best. Chip says get down and get right and take your medicine, and I like all of those better than riding the horse or taking the train or splitting the rails or slamming or banging or sticking or making good on a promise. I like riding horses and taking trains, and I don't like slamming or banging myself. Who the fuck knows what splitting the rails even means. Making good on a promise is too sad. It makes me think of Mary Poppins and piecrust promises, easily made and easily broken.

So I stick with what Chip says.

∽

Mack wants to make dinner, in honor of us having a kitchen. Chip has to stay at Felicity Street since people need to get their get-rights, especially around dinner time, and since Mack's doing the cooking, it's only fair I do the shopping. I walk right down the way to Zara's Grocery for pork chops and apples, potatoes and sour cream, bacon and green beans.

∽

While Mack makes dinner, Chip and I make foil envelopes. We each have a TV tray, like little drafting tables, we have our space to create. Chip says my hands are perfect, nimble—I'm the only one in this house with nails for making the creases and folds just right. Chip gives me an envelope for every twenty I fold, which is already saving us money. Mack is right about some things.

I can smell the apples getting soft in the kitchen and Chip winks at me.

"You wanna get right before dinner?"

"Of course."

"Just between you and me," he says, and winks again. Although I think winking is generally creepy, the way Chip does it seems harmless and silly, like he's making a joke instead of making a pass.

"Just between you and me," I repeat. "We don't want Mack burning our pork chops."

Chip takes a bag out of a cherrywood box that's sitting on top of his end table, like no one would see it there. He has a big spoon in there, too. Bigger than I use, almost like a ladle, but not quite that deep. I am sometimes shocked by how many kinds of spoons and knives there are in the world when my mother only had one kind of everything.

∾

We're all cooking all over the house.

Chip gets a line quick in his arm, he calls it Old Faithful, but I can't get anything. I have small arms and all my muscle tone lives in my legs. Arms are hard for me.

"Let me help you there, little chick," Chip says, and I am relieved. I don't always want to do this to myself, all by myself.

∾

See, I'm Chip's baby girl. I'm Chip's sugar hen. Sugar chick. We eat Raisinets and Blue Bell ice cream together and talk about when Orleans Parish was a place where people could get a little ahead. Sugar on sugar makes the bumps on my tongue get gritty. But I love it. I press the top of my tongue up and over, fold it back on the rest of my mouth so I can really smash the grit down and feel the sweetness.

Chip was the chief engineer for Copeland's ten years ago. Before Al Copeland lost his shit and got fucked in the media. Chip was servicing a boiler on the bottom floor of the Superdome when he fell off a twenty-two foot ladder and broke his back. It must've been pretty fucking frightening to fall from such heights. Four people tall.

Chip's mama, Suzette, was a nurse before she was a junky and after she was a junky too, in varying orders she'd been a nurse and a junky, but when Chip broke his back, she started in on him for his painkillers. He got laid off while he was on disability and the insurance stopped, so he went from pills to powder and got a divorce and lost the kids and then he started working at the Moonlight.

Chip already told me I could come into his room without knocking.

When Chip still worked at the Moonlight, before he made selling people sticky lumps and foil envelopes of powder his full-time job, and before I knew how to get a line by myself, Chip helped me every time.

Chip told me never to let anyone else touch my arms or rub hands over my veins, because nobody is as professional as Chip. Chip taught me how to be a perfectionist about this.

Chip taught me to un-cinch the belt before you take the needle out, to avoid a bruise. Chip taught me about pumping a fist to get a vein.

He taught me how to roll a cotton tight and always save a methadone wafer in a secret spot for a bad day.

You don't really need to slap skin to make a blue line pop.

How to pull up shallow, how to avoid dulling the needle, how to press it shallow in the vein.

Rub ash on the underbelly of a spoon to clean the smudge, catch the simmer before it boils, always shoot toward your heart.

He taught me about smiling at the boys on our set, who to make eye contact with, who to swing those hips for.

My arm feels safe inside Chip's hand. My head feels safe when it drops to his shoulder, when the cut's so good I nod out with the needle still in.

❧

My mother always said I was a perfectionist, too. The kind of kid who stayed up reading with a flashlight. The kind of kid who used a ruler to draw block letters for homemade birthday cards and who cried when she got a B+, because anything would be better than a B+, an F would be better than a B+.

I love the way I eat when I'm high. I eat like I talk, get every-thing I want, gobble quick, lick the plate and take seconds. I love real butter, yellow pressed into the crusty bread and the sauce dripping off my lips, caught. We drink soda water and I squeeze lemons, cut side up so the seeds don't drop, 'til it tastes like sparkling lemonade. We feast.

I know I fought Mack about moving here, but I think Felicity Street is going to be something good. Something right and delicious and I'm going to be safe here.

VI

Ra's been coming to the house every day, same time, same knock. It's nice to have some routine.

After he brings the delivery, Chip and I make the envelopes and Mack makes deliveries to the people who can't get by Felicity Street. We're a team.

I go to work, Mack goes to work, Chip mans the fort.

Today's delivery was so good, I feel like a petal floating down the street.

∾

I got cut from the Moonlight early today. Which is fine, I'd already run the bar tape and gotten enough cash to keep us through the night and into tomorrow. I picked up the night shift Tuesday. Mack'll get a payout and Chip'll front us something if our skin gets crawling, but now that we've moved here, we almost never crawl. Tonight I'll go home to Chip and keep it simple—just dope and wait 'til Mack gets off and then the three of us can get right, stay in, watch a movie.

Mack had to stay at the Moonlight, but he wants me to bring him back a piece. That's been his thing lately, little pieces at work, nothing to get too excited about, maintenance. Which is new. I think he's trying to show restraint since he's pretending we're going to Colorado soon. Saving money, being frugal.

Mack used to be frugal every day, but something changed when we started dating. When we first met, almost a year ago now, his eyes were thick, glassy lakes and I floated inside them, on top like a bubble. But he's not so glassy anymore; maybe I'm the glass now.

∾

Part of being frugal was not banging. When you use your nose, it lasts longer, so you buy less. Mack tried to impart the importance of this upon me. Mack told me never to bang. There aren't that many people who keep getting down as long as Mack has been. He's thirty-two. Not too many people who've never been arrested and who've always had a job— it's a point of great pride with Mack. He always claimed it was because he'd never banged. Then one day his nose stopped working. He bent down to blow a line, and nothing. I was there, I saw. Nothing would go up.

For a little while, he tried to keep buying the same amount, but it wears off quick when you bang. He must have noticed how much he's been using lately, gone back to being frugal. I understand. There are things we all believe are worth maintaining.

❧

I like being able to walk through the air like this. It's light and you could almost forget that we're situated at the downest part of the river, below the water even, like a mermaid city. I love that about here, I love it that we're down, makes me feel good when we talk about goin' down, gettin' down, takin' the train downtown, takin' a trip down to the bottom, makes me feel like I'm in the perfect right place to be right where I am.

The magnolia tree in front of the Moonlight started shedding today, little by little, white petals down, too. If I could be anything today I'd choose magnolia petal. But I'd be an up one. Prettier that way, makes people see delicate. Not that I'm delicate. Not that much.

❧

I'm thinking this is going to be perfect: Chip'll be at Felicity Street, I can get down nice and quick, run back to the Moonlight, give Mack his little piece, head back to nod. All before the sun goes all the way down. I'll probably get a kiss. If I ask nice.

❧

Hassan didn't even yell at me today, he didn't even tell me to clean anything twice, just smiled when he saw me like he used to, just looked at me and thought I was a pretty little petal, I think.

Zara's is busy, people getting their Andouille and dirty rice for dinner, but I go straight for the counter, get my cigarettes with no wait at all.

Man, look. Ra. Ra right there and I didn't even have to go looking. I call him and he smiles and looks me up and down like he likes to, all the way to my toes. I love the way he pronounces my name, like it's five syllables instead of one, like it's a whole long line of poetry. Look at him looking at me, what a catch. What a day. What a good batch of dope.

Ra asks me where I'm coming from and where I'm going. I don't go too many places, just around the neighborhood, just around the block. Who could feel trapped in a place like this, only if you felt trapped in a petal, maybe.

He tells me Chip wanted another delivery today, and Felicity Street is where he was headed, too. Down the street, he even touches my neck, pulls the little hairs sticking out from my braid and brushes up against my arm like he doesn't know he's doing it.

Ra laughs when I tell him I'm happy to see him, like no one's ever told him that before, though I know everybody who sees Ra is happy to see him.

We walk into Chip's room and I hear her before I see her, Chip's mama Suzette's here. Ra sighs like he wasn't planning on being too long. Everybody knows when Suzette's here, Chip's agitated. Chip has a whole routine to get him done with being agitated. Ra knows and I know, and I don't think either of us wants to wait around. Ra's got deliveries to make and I've got places to float. I need to get back to Mack and the Moonlight. If anyone can un-agitate Chip, it's me.

❧

Chip calls his bedroom the king's room, and he even has a leopard print comforter, pillows with gold tassels hanging off them. Someone traded him for it. I hope Chip stops taking all this trade, the house is getting full and word's going to start getting around that you can get an envelope for a porcelain figurine or a comforter. You can't pay the rent in trade.

Even after we call his name a couple times it doesn't seem like Chip can hear us, so Ra leads us into the living room. I'm behind Ra, and he's big, so big his whole body covers my whole body and I think what would it be like if his body was really covering mine, like a comforter covering me, but I stop. That's not right. Nobody's supposed to cover me but Mack.

Suzette's on the couch and Chip's standing in front of her, and they're both talking at the same time, like they're gonna be able to hear each other not listening.

"Mama just needs a little one more piece, bebe. Just a little one more."

"What'd you want, ma? You want one more, here fucking take it."

❧

It's alright on top of each other. Like Ra might be on top of me if we were horizontal instead of vertical. Mack's waiting for me back at the Moonlight and I was hoping to get back before the sun went down, when there'd still be a little light out and I could remember what a beautiful great petal day it is.

Chip throws a dollar at Suzette and tells her to take the bus, but it doesn't seem like she wants to do that at all.

"Don't do that to your mama, bebe. With the people here. Callin' your mother a shit. A pathetic shit, I didn't raise you to be like this."

"Thank you, thank you! People! For the luvva god, people! Look at this pathetic shit. This is my mother, say hi Ma, say hi to the people."

Suzette looks at us and gives a little wave, just a brush of her hand, and Ra tells Chip he has some more errands to run. Chip looks at Suzette and almost spits, then gives me a kiss on the head and holds my hand and leads us both back to the king's room.

"Thank god you're both here, Jesus shit, my mother."

∾

Ra weighs out some big sticky lumps and I'm so happy, the day's back to beautiful and I might just make it back to the Moonlight before sunlight's gone, be a good girlfriend to Mack and maybe by the time I come back Suzette will have finally gotten her piece and gone to the bus stop. After Ra gives Chip his lumps, enough to keep us (and a lot of other people) well all night and all day tomorrow, he gives me a special piece and smiles and tells me he's glad I'm around here more often, I'm a pretty little thing in this place. I am.

Suzette's making moaning sounds from the couch and Chip won't stop talking about how much she's agitating him. I tell him there's a cure for everything right here in front of us and we get right, sitting on the leopard print comforter.

I sink in real good, like I'm a dot on a big cat, a spot in the wild, I'm inside it. A petal is light and a dot is dark but I'm both and I get to float and sink and I know Mack really loves me. He really, really loves me, and so does Chip.

There is a dying cow on our couch. My mother says you shoot a dying animal, but my father says we don't have a gun. Why is there a cow on our couch? We are in the city.

Chip's standing up facing me, knees bent, one arm hanging on the TV tray by the bed, the other arm straight in front of him, his eyes closed, just a little wetness at the corner of his mouth. There's a slow, low bounce in his knees, like he's about to take off. I've got to let him know about the death of livestock.

"Chip. Chip."

"What, I'm awake."

I ask him what's happening in the living room. I tell him Mack needs a little piece, I'm supposed to go back and give it to him. Chip dips low before he straightens up, looks like he's going to drop all the way down to the carpet. I've never even seen a house in this city with carpet. But it's probably better for us, soft.

I follow Chip into the living room and Suzette's eyes are closed, but I don't know if she's sleeping, she's the one making the sounds. She's the cow. She's making a noise like she's running out of breath and Chip shakes her really hard.

And then he opens his palm and slams it on her eye, slams it over and over again, then slams it some more. I don't know what to say, there's not a dying cow on our couch, it's Chip's mom, and he's punching her now, closed fist, throwing it on her head, and I might be a little scared because he's yelling things like she's a bitch and a whore and when she wakes up she's going to remember this and he's going to make sure she remembers this. Remember when she taught him how to do this, look how fucking well she taught him to bring her motherfucking back.

And she's back. The way she comes back is like an old lady waking up from a nap, she opens her eyes real slow, not from a nod but from a deep, deep dream where you expect the waking world to be just like the one you've left, like the one where everything's red and lush and thick.

He's still yelling at her and throws another dollar at her and pulls her by her orange t-shirt and tells her she's gonna miss her bus, get the fuck out.

She leaves. It doesn't look like she sees me, but her face is puffed up like a jellyfish and her lip looks like the inside of a grape. I want to cry but instead I remember Mack and realize I don't know how much time has passed. I need to get back to the Moonlight, there's no more sun to get there quick with. Chip's breathing heavy, but not like a cow, not like his mother, just like he's a man very tired and very agitated. I tell him again Mack needs a piece and he grumbles and goes into the room and breaks off a piece of down and shoves it into my palm.

∾

Back on the street I float again, I breathe again, it was a little suffocating in that house with Chip and Suzette and all those cow noises. I like to breathe, except it reminds me of Suzette, and I don't want to have anything in common with her.

There are pretty things in this place, not just dark down apartments and dogs tied up with chains. There are things like me and things like the trees that line the street all covered in petals and blossoms. We need a tree in that apartment. Sometimes the petal side of me gets to wishing it was a little softer, a little lighter around here, but the sun is going down, it's almost dark and I need to get back to the Moonlight. I can feel the glass starting to cover my eyes like a shell, like a protective layer against the things I'd rather not see. Suzette is lumpy and folded and even though I have gotten out of there, she seems stuck inside my eye. And so I let that glass break, maybe if I can cry, she will leak out, maybe she will disappear.

I duck back behind the big live oak by Zara's and squat down and cry. The air is so damp here, just like my cheeks, I make my skin match the air and think of how that means I can be a floating part of it. I feel immaculate when that thin little border between me and the air, me and everything else breaks and I become more like something else, something other than me.

VII

November 2, and I wake up crying. I know this is a bad omen, one I cannot shake even as Mack and I walk to the polls down Magazine Street. We stop for a drink at Ms. Mae's before casting our lackluster Kerry ballots. We leave quietly. Mack has taught me enough about politics that I know when not to discuss them. We have another drink on the way home and head to the Moonlight to punch in and watch the returns roll.

❧

Warring is getting worse, and Jennifer tried to kick out all the prostitutes at the Josephine Street place, but they ganged up on her, she says, told her they had just as much right to be there as she did. So Jennifer and Chip borrow Mumps' car and load Warring into the backseat in a bathrobe. He takes a spot on the plaid couch. Warring smells like licorice and coconut and pus. I don't think anyone thought to take him to vote today.

❧

Election night is almost as bad as Ivan, with the one-note conversations and a two-deep bar, but at least these two-deeps are regulars, neighborhood people. The ladies from the park have a little bounce in their step, like there's something that could happen tonight that could mean something, even if it never touches us. We all know that D.C. is a long way from the Delta and that shit flows downstream anyway. At least we have something to talk about.

∿

"You can't blame people for not being enthused about this guy, he doesn't have much charisma," the girl drinking whiskey soda with bitters says.

I think enthused is a very matronly word for a girl her age to be using.

"It's an immature position," her older male companion says, "considering what's at stake."

I wonder if they sleep together. He owns the dark room next door.

"And voting for the more handsome candidate is somehow more mature?"

"It's apples and oranges," he says. "Finish your drink. This is over. Bush has it."

"But California's not back," she says. "I want another drink."

"Even if California, Oregon and Washington all went for Kerry, however unenthusiastically, he'd still lose. But stay for another drink if you want. I'm exhausted."

He leaves and she stays for three more drinks, asking for more and more bitters each time.

❧

Warring says this is the first time in thirty-two years he hasn't voted. The only other time he was eligible but abstained was 1968. "The whole thing was a shit-show," he says, "I'm damn near sure my brother voted for Wallace, and I couldn't stomach it to even go to the damn booth with him."

❧

Warring has cast his ballot in favor of:
George McGovern
Jimmy Carter
Ronald Reagan (twice)
Michael Dukakis
Bill Clinton (twice)
Ralph Nader

❧

"I even voted when I was in Vietnam," he says, "they passed out ballots to all of us, who knows if they got counted, but they sure made a big show of the whole thing. Big fucking production."

Warring is one of the few people who I genuinely believe enjoys chicory coffee. I make it for him and run to Zara's because the milk is in chunks. Warring appreciates the little things we do for him. It makes me sad to see him so grateful for unspoiled milk.

∾

"I knew something horrible was going to happen," I say.

"Well it didn't take a clairvoyant to figure that one out," Mack says.

"You don't think the tears were the least bit prescient?"

"You wake up crying every other day. What's the omen there?" he asks.

∾

Things Mack and I fight about:
   My college friends
   My Marigny friends
   My dude friends
   My friendship with Chip
   My friendship with Jennifer
   My insistence that Hemingway is not the greatest American writer of all time
   The profundity of punk rock
   Boulder
   The gold standard
   Dishes
   Ice trays
   My friendship with Mumps
   The importance of a college degree

The wisdom of having moved to Felicity Street
Ra's intentions regarding my ass
Hassan's intentions regarding my ass
Whether or not I should spend any time at The Saint
The definition of junky
The moral imperative of kindness

∾

Jennifer bought a typewriter, presumably to keep working on this novel she keeps talking about, says she's been working on it for ten years, but I never see her type shit. She took it out of its case the first night she had it, showed it off to everyone and since then it's been Warring's footrest. His feet are so swollen they don't fit into his house slippers. Thank god he can still pull socks over them. It's particularly troublesome because his ankles were the only place he could get right. Jennifer tries to find small places in his wrists, but they're so bony it hurts. I have to walk out of the room when she uses his jugular.

∾

My mother thinks Thanksgiving is the most important of the holidays and I tell her I will come home, if I can get the days off.

"What kind of establishment is open on Thanksgiving? Don't people have families in that city?" she asks.

Of course we have families, I think. That's why we stay open—so we can spend the holidays with our family.

∽

Warring asks if I know how to make oyster stuffing, which I don't, but Chip claims he has a family recipe. I hope it's not Suzette's. There are big plans for Thanksgiving at Felicity Street. Chip says he wants to shoot a turkey, although that seems dangerous and far-fetched. He won't stop talking about it.

∽

For these things, I am grateful:
>The way Chip smiles when I walk in the door
>Mack in a good mood
>Control-top panty hose
>That I live in the most alive place in the world
>Not hearing my mother's fork scraping against the plate moving food and not eating it
>The sourness of a cranberry
>The millions of veins in the body
>Mascara
>Graph paper
>Having a place of our own, with a kitchen, where we don't have to pretend not to nod

∽

Since my grandparents on both sides helped build Our Lady of Perpetual Hope, there were always priests around during the holidays. Grace was protracted, especially on secular holidays like Thanksgiving. The priests always went through the buffet first, then the adults and then the kids.

One year when Father O'Brien was late, as I was taking the last roll, my mother snatched it from my plate, a little line of gravy outlining the bottom, and threw it back in the basket so there'd be something left when he arrived.

"You don't need that starch, anyway," she said, "would it kill you to put a little salad on that plate? My god, every meal looks like your last."

"It's Thanksgiving," I said.

"Your plate always looks like Thanksgiving."

❧

Someone traded Chip a remote-controlled boat for a bag and he and Mack take off to find a place to play, leaving me and Warring the house to ourselves.

Warring tells me about Ting-Ting from Vietnam, the prettiest woman he's ever seen. He tells me why we call our syringes 'outfits.' It's what the guys in Vietnam made up when they got dope habits over there—all syringes look the same, like army-issue outfits. And he tells me about the Ironworkers Union, how it's the most corrupt thing he's ever been a part of, next to the United States Army. Warring always wears his St. Sebastian medal, patron saint of iron-workers (and unruly children).

"All these junkies coming through here every day, got more integrity than the whole lot of 'em in the union," he says.

"I don't know about that, Warring, you see what these people are like."

"At least they don't make qualms about what they're here for," he says. "Some people just don't got nothing else they could be doing. But that ain't you, Claire, you're prolly the only one keepin' on airs 'bout what you're here for."

"What do you mean?" I feel badly for asking him questions since it takes him such effort to talk.

"Now don't go playin' all dumb on me now, makin' like pretty's all you got. Sweet girl, Claire, cleaning up all the time, and talkin' to Chip and makin' coffee. I know why the rest of 'em are here, but you don't need to be wasting your time gettin' me milk and listenin' to stories about ironworkers. You ain't got shit to know about workin' iron and there are plenty people in the world besides Chip to talk to. "

"What are you talking about? I like hearing your stories. I love you guys."

"I don't love you, Claire. I think you're real nice, and you're a real smart girl, but if you think this shit's love, you're not as smart as I thought."

I wish he would stop wasting his breath on me, the way it pushes out, it seems he's got so little left.

∾

I press myself so hard into Mack I think he's going to break and I make myself so wide open I think I'm going to split.

∾

The grand plans for Thanksgiving turn into rotisserie chicken, Stovetop and Stouffer's macaroni and cheese. But I'm on the schedule at the Moonlight, so I get all those generous, lonely tippers. I let Chip give us all our medicine for free on account of the holiday and start an envelope labeled "Boulder," slip it under my jeans in the top drawer.

∾

Even though there's no snow, I get us an advent calendar. It's not just for chocolate, it's the countdown to the mountains. 2005 is going to be a year of high and dry.

∾

The money comes in and out of that fucking envelope like the people in and out of this house Warring thinks are so damn principled.

∾

My mother sends a card: Santa's sad you won't be home for Christmas. Frowny face. Sorry you have to work. We'll have to plan a trip down soon. We love you.

I cash the $100 check at the Magazine Discount Corner Store and put the whole thing in my Boulder envelope. And for a second, I feel a little piercing in my tummy.

∾

It snows on Christmas for the first time in twenty years. We try to make a snowman, but there's not much more than watery snowflakes on our tongues. We open presents in the living room. Jennifer puts a green and red plaid blanket over Warring's feet and we drink hot apple cider.

"Everybody go get a sock," Chip says, and we comply.

Gold-toe heather grey, black and white polka dot, nubby forest green. I don't own a pair of socks, so Jennifer gives me the match to the polka dotted left and Chip walks around the room on his tip-toes dropping pieces of down into what he calls our stockings.

"Have you been a good egg or a bad egg?" he asks us and gives us each a nuzzle with his nose.

∾

There is no need for me to make a list of resolutions because I'm making resolutions every day. All the time, all of us, we're always resolving to change it up.

∾

I take down the lights at Felicity Street, just one strand I hung above our doorway. My father always said you aren't supposed to take the lights down or haul the tree to the curb until Epiphany, but I've had so many, I don't think the rule applies.

∾

VIII

I hate when Suzette is at the house, but Chip says Suzette has nothing to do with me and I should just be grateful she isn't my mother. Chip doesn't eat peanuts because when he was little she used to make him clean out the bathtub after she tried to kick, after she would shit all over the bathtub. He says no matter how hard he scrubbed, that thing was always the color of peanut shells.

But Suzette is at Felicity Street almost every day. I ask Hassan for more hours at work.

∽

I've been asking around and everyone has a different strategy for kicking:

Nyquil, soup and Gatorade
Ice cream with a Vicodin mix-in
Thera-Flu
A tiny bit of methadone and constant masturbation
The best pot you can find and a bottle of whiskey
A big fucking lock or a shotgun

Jail
Jennifer told me reading helps

∽

Jennifer rubs Warring's feet and when his sister from Iowa calls, she gives her updates. Felicity Street is full.

∽

The best part of every night at the Moonlight is Mumps.

Mumps' real name is Sydney Dobner, but everybody calls him Mumps. There's Mumps, the person. Then there's Mumpsie, his band. But both names originate from Mumpsie the Cat, this mangy skittery alley tabby that jumped around Uptown when Mumps and I lived next door to each other on Oak Street.

Mumps and I spent a lot of Oak Street dollars together.

∽

This is an Oak Street Dollar:
25¢ can of Budweiser
50¢ shot of Hot Damn!
25¢ tip

∽

There are two bars on Oak Street: Snake and Jake's Christmas Club (the more patronized of the two) and S&J's

Lounge. Both involve the Oak Street dollar. All day, people walk up and down Oak Street, asking folks on their porches if they can bum an Oak Street dollar. If you acquiesce, it's customary to escort the person in, buy the drinks, and tip the quarter yourself, but if you choose to stay on your porch and just fork over a buck, it's still safe to assume the bartender will receive that quarter tip.

Mumps and I share a weakness: the inability to say no.

I wonder how many Oak Street dollars we could have saved by being no people.

∽

At the Moonlight it's all glass, water, soap, glass, metal, aluminum, metal on metal, ceramic on skin, cellophane and paper and busted ink pens, glass and dust and glass and glass and glass and ice. Then there's some time to sit in the corner on a barstool. And then it starts again. Napkin, glass, ice, liquid, paper/plastic.

I might eat some Raisinets. Order some hummus from the back. Puke it up and start over. Sometimes I keep a spoon tucked into the sleeve of my sweater. I think Steve-D is the only one who notices because he's started scowling at me.

Steve-D is the tallest person at the Moonlight, has to duck his head to cross the threshold between the dining room and the kitchen. He's always reminding everyone that he's not actually on the Moonlight payroll.

I'm an independent contractor, so don't tell me I need to mop the damn floor, somebody who's on the payroll can do that shit, he'll say. Steve-D is a delivery driver. I've never known if his last name starts with D, or if D is for delivery. He's worked here since the place opened, and he thinks that counts as a good thing.

He used to smile at me, we used to smoke pot in the courtyard between deliveries, share opinions about candy, but lately he just seems prejudiced, narrow-minded, like he can't see the universality of habit. My spoon up a sleeve's not so different than his pipe in a pocket.

Mumps is sitting on the last barstool, corner, beside the video poker. He's folding a napkin into triangles, small and smaller, then punts it between the Abita and Sam Adams taps. I napkin him, glass and ice him, ask him what sort of liquid I should pour and he wants pineapple juice if I have it. I have it. I like the pineapple juices, too—the miniature cans make it taste better. He slides his Discover card toward me.

"What's on your tab so far?" he asks. I let Mumps pay part of the night's open bar tab with his credit card whenever he wants, give him the cash back. I'm sure we're not the ones who made this scam up, but we sure do feel smart.

"It's pretty big, Happy Hour was busy. What do you want?"

"Two?" He looks typically unsure of himself, letting the hair fall from behind his ears to cover his face like curtains.

I check the computer, we've already sold $679 worth of booze and it's not even ten. Two hundred won't look suspicious at all, not that there's anyone to be suspicious of anything around here. I run the card and count ten twenties. Mumps gives one back.

"You realize that's only a ten percent tip," I say and raise my eyebrows, "plus the juice."

Mumps smiles and asks for a go-cup. I tell him to just take the glass. One less to wash.

It's funny that Mumps is the one person from Tulane I still hang out with, because we were never much in the same scene then. But now, Mumps and I are bridges between people for each other. Now when one of us needs to make an appearance Uptown, we'll go with each other, stay for a beer or two before we book it back to the Channel and get right. It doesn't matter if it's one of his metal shows or one of my hippie parties. One thing this city is good for is mingling. Especially Mumps—Mumps'll be awkward and anxious around anyone just the same. So he's awkward and anxious, but he's honest. I've never met someone so stupidly honest — clean, straight, young, old—this kid couldn't lie to a kindergartner. It's his downfall, really.

Like with the Discover card. Mumps' parents gave him a credit card as a graduation gift. Stupid. But then again, they know their kid, know he's honest. I guess they intended it to be a safety net until he got his career together. I heard back in May, at one of those Mimosa-and-Bellini, cap-and-gown parties that it had a $50,000 limit, which seems like it would last a while. But those cash advances go quick.

Mumps never needed to tell anyone about that credit card. If it was mine, I sure fucking wouldn't, but when people are broke and asking everybody for ten, twenty bucks to float 'em 'til tomorrow, Mumps is always the one who says, yeah, yeah, I got the card. So now everybody knows he's the one.

Chip knows about the card. Whenever he needs re-up money, a little front, he goes to Mumps. Mumps is scared of being sick. Everybody knows that, and if Chip makes it seem like we're all gonna be sick if we don't get some cash together, Mumps is the first one to jump in and volunteer the front. Fucked up thing is that Chip'll take the money, get a grip, divvy it up, sell some pieces, make Mumps' money back, get straight with Mumps and then sell him pieces at full price. Sometimes I buy extras for Mumps since Chip gives me the family discount. It's fucked that Mumps doesn't get the discount when he's actually the one buying the shit in the first place, but I'm not in charge of those things.

Because he's scared of getting sick, Mumps tries to buy in bulk. Methadone wafers and Oxys, Vics, anything that might work in an emergency. That could be part of the credit card problem, too. But he's not stingy about it—he likes to be hero for the day—the front-money man, the warehouse, an emergency wafer here or there to someone. I don't know if he thinks of it all as an investment—if everything is done in case of emergency, a favor done today to ensure a favor owed tomorrow—or if he really wants to feel as though we're all in this together.

∽

"You want me to order you something from Chip?" Mumps asks before he takes off.

"No, I'm done."

"You're leaving? You want me to just wait for you?"

"No, I'm done with this shit."

I tell Mumps about Suzette and Chip and how not-tough I really am. How I'm more like a petal than anything else. How I'm sick of being sick every fucking morning, how sometimes I don't get out of bed, just call Chip's name and have him give me my first dose, let it wait to kick in good before I brush my teeth. Pathetic.

"I'm going to Boulder," I say. "The election's over."

"I'm done soon, too," Mumps says. He's an awful liar.

∽

I'll be able to get to Boulder in a couple weeks. I'm going to move out of Felicity Street, Mumps will let me stay at his place and save the month's rent. If Mack can't kick with me, he'll just have to meet me there. Or not.

❧

Monday, Tuesday, Wednesday are the slow days at the bar, so I tell Hassan I have to go to Texas because my sister is sick, take me off the schedule for three days. This is for real. I mean it. I'm sticking it out. I'm moving through it. I'm resolved and ready and this is really going to be for real.

❧

From my list of kick strategies, I choose reading—The Heart is a Lonely Hunter. And whiskey—Evan Williams.

It's not surprising that Jennifer told me reading helps. Last week, she laid on my mattress, having a bad day, one of those days you think a kick might actually be better than doing the same fucking thing one more time, and she told me again about her novel.

I could see the wrinkles that are usually invisible, or at least covered up with her thick-tipped kohl and falsies. The way Jennifer wears falsies, they don't look like Tammy Faye Baker, they look devastating, like she was born in go-go boots and blue eye shadow and a hint of glitter threaded through those thick blonde streaks. But with her eyes squinted, and the make-up falling off her face, she looked almost old. People regularly take Jennifer for younger than I am, she's carded down in the Quarter. She says it's the drugs. They've pickled her.

∾

There are craters in my brain, big open gashes howling feed me feed me feed me like there's some kind of small animal that swam up from my belly and into my head. Like it doesn't know words, just full and empty and it won't stop scritching. I thought I'd killed that thing.

∾

Opioid receptors are permanent. Chip has explained it all, he is an expert. Everyone has them, but most people never use them. Most people keep those receptor doors locked, but we flung them open. We have wide drafty gaps. And right now, the wind is blowing in sharp sub-zero, coming over me in waves. I'm shivering even though I'm under the blankets. The cheap leopard print covers crawl on my skin, I can't touch anything, least of all myself. To masturbate through this is insane. I can't touch my hair to put it in a ponytail, much less rub circles on my clit.

∾

I try to make lists in my head, even if I can't bring myself to find my notebook. Anything to keep my mind off Chip bundling envelopes. I try to name fruits, and the only thing I can think of is cantaloupe. Cowardly, cowardly cantaloupe.

∾

I go back and forth, covered in the crawling blankets, wishing my skin itched from the dope instead of the scratchy fabric, then I'm freezing, burning again, pushing the blankets to the floor, sweating, I'm burning, burning off the bone. My knees are sweating. And then back to freezing, lowering my arm for the blanket, like I've been pumped full of cemented jerky, like I'm Warring in the hospital.

But I have a book. And I'm reading, trying to read, looking through the pages.

∾

The back and forth subsides and I can smoke a little Afghani and drink a little sip of Evan Williams and hope the wave will last. I feel like I could sit up and make a phone call or walk to the bathroom or turn the page in the book, that's when my mind starts in, and what passes for logic starts churning. Chip's right there. No point in going cold turkey, no one's done that since the 70s. You've already started to wean. Then the rehab stuff starts to morph. We didn't become addicted in one day, so easy does it. That's right. Easy does it, I shouldn't try to get clean in one day. How about one bag a day? One bag a day is affordable. One bag a day is totally acceptable. Totally workable. Totally totally what I should do. That's what I'll do. One bag a day. Then half a bag a day. Then a shot a day. Then I'll move to Nicaragua and teach English and smoke hash on the beach. That's what will happen. One bag a day. It's almost like one day at a time. That's the most reassuring part of the whole bullshit. Seems like the way I already operate—the way we all operate. I'm practically in recovery already. One bag at a time.

❧

Scritch. Scritch. Scritch-scritch. I'm still in this fucking bed in this fucking house where I will never ever be able to leave. But I love it here. I'm lucky to be here. I mean it.

❧

"Don't you look like you've looked hotter," Jennifer says as she sits on the edge of the bed, blanket splayed half on, my leg crooked in between. "Smells like a kick in here." She is referring to the stench of my sweat and the vomit I have left in the toilet and the poison that is draining from my pores—it smells like sewage. I didn't vomit from the lack of dope; I vomited from the smell of myself.

❧

I quit:
    Girl Scouts
    Soccer
    Voice Lessons
    Eating beef
    Not eating beef
    National Honor Society

❧

Jennifer asks if I want a backrub. Her touching my skin, the thought of my own skin touching my own bones, is disgusting. Jennifer asks if I want a shot and I cry. All the fluids sucked dry to the dope start to pour. The only thing I have felt more than sick or well for months are the occasional rushes of perfection when the cut is just right and I have waited just long enough—not so long that I am sick, but not so quick the dope is redundant. And now, with this pickled woman perched on the edge of my bed, I cannot control the flooding.

"I just want to go to the mountains," I say over and over again. "I just want to get the fuck out of this place."

Jennifer crawls over me, becomes part of the leopard, she lifts my head and lowers it to her lap, lets me sob into the space between her thighs. Jennifer gathers my sticky hair, matted at the scalp, tangled and pressed together, I have not brushed in weeks. She twists the long strands of my honeypoppy hair into a thick knot and presses circles into my temples, like it's my clit. I can breathe again.

∾

"You want a get-down, baby," she says like it's a bite of ice cream for a sick child, like it's a bottle for a baby, she says it and it's the only thing in the whole world I want more than her holding me. It's all I need in the world to happen.

I say, "I'm kicking. I'm going to Colorado, I need my ticket. Where's my ticket?" I wonder if this would be easier on a bus, where I couldn't cry and I couldn't lay down and I couldn't get my temples rubbed by a pretty pickled lady.

∾

I have run out of lines and holes. My arms are bloated and fresh open with bright red and deep purple and my legs are delicate yellow green, the color of hay in the sunlight. It hurts to wear pants. And it hurts to wear shirts. And my nose is out of the question and has been for a year. I've become a disgusting mouth-breather.

❧

"I'll help you," she says, and yes, yes, I think, that's what I need, I need some help.

"You want a get-down, baby," she repeats, and I know yes. If she can help me find a place, surely she can also help me get dressed. There's a lot to be said for this effort I've made. My tolerance is down already. Easy does it.

Jennifer goes to Chip's room and returns with a piece, cooks it for me on the floor.

"Where's your outfit?"

I can't muster words, just point to the top dresser drawer.

"The one with the ribbon?" she asks.

I always tie my favorite piece of ribbon to the outfit that's the sharpest and least bent. Even if all outfits do look the same, I make sure mine are identified with ribbon, girl.

❧

Things I will never quit:
    Swimming

❧

She pulls my tank top off slowly, like she'll kiss my nipples next, and cups my left breast in her long fingers. Her chipped peach fingernails brush over my veins, I have never noticed the road from nipple to heart.

"You'll feel better in one minute, this is a secret, baby, this is a girl secret, clutch, I'm gonna teach you this, right like this."

I love her. She pinches my nipple with her fingernails and it feels perfect, like it was born inside her hand and like magic a thin blue road pops. She presses the tip in toward my heart, so shallow I can feel the metal on the down side of my skin, quick pulls up the register and there it is red and gone in less than a second.

A button the size of a tiny pill rises at the outside of my areola, swells then drains and shrinks, passing the dope onward. My head is still between her legs and I can smell her, she smells like dope and chamomile, pussy and ciga-rettes and lilac and I love her, I love her for this. I press my face into the place between her thighs and breathe her in and she strokes my hair and says, "That's my girl, feel better now, don't worry, you'll do this, we're all gonna do it."

I'm for real, I'm going to do it, it's almost like I already have.

༄

I sink in real good, there's that spot in the wild feeling, I'm inside it. Her pussy is light and a dot is dark but I'm both and I get to float and sink and I know right here is the place I was meant to love someone, Jennifer loves me. It's just like those petals.

I feel the dope moving through my body, down to my toes, not quite, but soon, two directions at once, which is new. Usually dope travels in one direction, towards your heart, and then, slower, it radiates out, you are the sun. Sometimes it moves so slowly you can barely register it, but this is happening in two directions at once and I can't move, I just stay right where I am.

I look at Jennifer and see how she has done this so long and so well, how she gets people to love her. I love her because she loves me like this. I need a novel like hers. A novel like that would sustain me. A novel like hers would be a love story just like this.

∾

IX

No matter how many people leave, and there are always people leaving—people leaving to go to rehab, leaving to pull a geographic, leaving to serve sentences or evade arrest, evade child support, evade an ex or a debt or a dealer—there are always more to take their places on the couch and floor and kitchen counter.

This morning a girl wearing cat ears was nodding into our dish rack. Rude. I wonder if she's here for Mardi Gras.

Chip says this is no shooting gallery, this is a quick in-and-out, no fix, no tricks, a business place. But Chip can't stand to tell a pretty girl that. Or a man with money, or his mother, or his brother, or anyone. Chip's a sucker for a little ass-kissing. Chip's a talker. He'll bullshit all day long with the biggest bullshitters on the block. Hens.

❧

Another reason to leave New Orleans: the idiocy and inconvenience of the shotgun floor plan.

Mack and I have the room by the bathroom. In and out and through all day, people saying they just have to take a quick piss, come out with ant eyes. Mack has the balls to tell them no, but I can't stand to dictate the rules. It seems so hypocritical to get self-righteous about territory. But I don't have to let them lean on my bed. Like Chip only lets certain people in his room, I only let certain people lean. Mostly just Jennifer and Mumps. I'd let Warring lean too, if Warring could ever get vertical off the couch.

∾

Ra's shit's been so good people are falling out. Dope is the only drug where the best shit is the shit that lets you die just a little—to die just a little is what everybody brags about. The more you die and come back, the more you believe it'll never kill you. Another good reason not to let people in our bathroom.

∾

I take the long way to work to see how the carnival crowds are doing. A grown woman pushes a little girl down for a strand of fat, purple beads. I offer my hand and she says, "That was my daddy on the float. Those were my beads."

∾

Delivery this morning was early, and I was the only one awake when Ra knocked. Mack at work, I passed the cat ears and Warring on the plaid couch and Jennifer on the orange couch and Chip splayed on top of his big bed like a bat, opened the door and Ra smiled real big, like I was the only thing he wanted to see.

"Look who's the early bird," he said, "look who gets the worm, girl."

And I did. We went back to my room and I let Ra sit on our bed, and crossed my legs to hide the bruise on my thigh. I like Ra to think I've got it together.

Drug dealers are together, especially ones with as much business as Ra. They aren't all scumbags. Ra takes his nephews to the barber shop every Thursday after school, all six of them. I've walked past and seen him reading *Vibe* while they get their fades.

"You know I've been lookin' 'n seein' you lately, huh?" Ra's shirt looked incredibly starched, and I wondered if he has all his clothes dry cleaned.

"You can look all you want." I smiled, like I was enjoying it. And I was.

"But not touch, huh? You got that man."

"You know."

"Do I?"

"You're the one who said it, you must know. I've got a man."

"Well, you ever need some more worms, you know where to find 'em. You keep this lagniappe for you," he broke off a piece of sticky black tar, held it out. When I reached to take it, he pulled back, winked, "Come a little closer, I ain't gonna bite." I stood up and walked slow in a needlessly long arc around the room until I stood in front of him and leaned in close, plucked it from his palm and made sure to give a nice view. "You make sure that's just for you, ya hear."

"I hear."

∾

Other Early Birds of New Orleans:
    Cordilleran Flycatcher
    Cooper's Hawk
    Yellow-nosed Albatross
    Bard's Sandpiper
    Spicy Fried Chicken

I'm in good company.

∾

When Chip finally woke up, I knew that things had changed a little between us because I gave him the day's delivery, minus my private piece, and he didn't look proud of me the way I thought he would.

"You shoulda woke me up," he said.

"Ra was in a hurry."

"Come on," Chip said, "help me divvy this shit. He says it's a new batch. We gotta run a test."

∾

Testing is about determining the amount of quinine to add to powder. I am perfect for testing because I have equal and opposing allegiances. I won't let the cut get too strong, because I genuinely care about Chip and I won't let the cut get too weak, because I genuinely care about Mumps and Mack and Jennifer and Warring and of course, myself.

I cook and get a taste inside.

"Good," I say. Chip blows on my eyes. I revise my statement to "strong." Sometimes I think I can hear my pupils shrinking. Chip is up close to my eyes, like he will be able to tell just by looking—one more pinch, one more drip.

We separate the package into two pieces—one much larger than the other. To the smaller piece, we mix a 2:1 cut. To the larger piece a 3:1 cut. Then we portion everything out into foil envelopes.

"'Member to keep the three-to-ones separate from our good stuff," Chip says. Like I could ever forget.

∾

I got a coconut my very first Zulu, a high heel at my very first Muses. When the people come in carrying their parade bounty, I smirk and think about how hard they've worked for their piddly light-up crown beads and their dirty pouches of Bacchus wine. Throws are like anything else—you've got to act like you've already got it in order to actually get it.

Someone should tell these people you can order something besides a Bloody Mary, we won't take offense.

༄

16, 17, 18. I can hear Mumps counting from the other room. Mumps read somewhere that all overdoses happen within 25 seconds of intake. He adds another second to be safe. Mumps is always trying to be safe. Never shares outfits, and even so, is always rinsing his out with bleach. Keeps an eyedropper of bleach in his pocket, like it's Sucrets. But I guess that's ritual. Nobody can say we don't love ritual. It's like going to church, we believe in the things we repeat. Mumps believes in counting to 26 like Mack believes in masturbation and George W. believes in WMDs. 24, 25, 26.

Today Mumps and I are going Uptown to get rid of some stuff. The pawnshops up there give better buy prices, less competition. He's got tons of equipment—mixers and subwoofers, but today all we're taking is a bebe amp and a couple old pedals. I'm grateful we have a mission to escape the crowd that's accumulated through the morning. Mumps said he wanted some company, but I know he won't say two words the whole way there. One thing I like about Mumps: you can always be quiet around him and it still doesn't feel like there's nothing going on.

༄

I want to take the streetcar instead of Mumps' car, it's such a nice day, but Mumps says that doesn't make any sense at all, we'd have to carry all the shit on and off the streetcar and down to the pawnshop.

"I'll carry it, then," I say.

"You're being unreasonable, Claire."

"You're being unreasonable," I say back to him. "It's a gorgeous day. When was the last time you actually took the streetcar?"

"There's a reason I don't take that thing," he says. "It's the most inefficient means of transit we've got."

"Rickshaws? What about rickshaws," I say, winning.

Mumps rolls his eyes.

∾

Mumps is the worst negotiator I've ever seen. The woman offers him fifty bucks and he takes it so quick I almost expect him to offer forty-five.

∾

We've still got a little bit of nod left from the morning when we're done with the pawnshop so we stop at Audubon Park to lie in the grass under the live oaks and feel the roots push into our spines. Mumps says we're going to stop soon, that he's got a job lined up, a contact from the music business, that Grace is going to kick him out, that he knows Chip rips him off. He can't stand to look like the rich college kid sucker all the time.

Mumps wants to make a list of reasons why we should quit, but that's where I draw the line—there's no need to inventory the obvious. I prefer lists used for reference and planning, not directives, but description.

We watch a class of co-eds lead each other around the park blindfolded, touching the grass and bark and soil. We shit-talk the sorority girls tanning on their Green Wave blankets and pretend not to notice the middle-aged moms smoking a joint behind a tree, watching their toddlers slide and swing like monkeys. This place cracks me up.

"If you don't want to make a list of reasons to kick, we should at least make a list of things we believe in. You know, things we know for sure."

"Oh. My. God. That's literally from O Magazine. "

He looks so hurt, like I just kicked his little cat face.

"Sorry, I don't mean to be mean, I just mean," I try to apologize.

"No. I get it. You can't make a list of things you believe in if you don't believe in anything."

He looks satisfied and I'm proud of him.

∽

The streetcar is packed. I hadn't thought about the tourists.

"Beautiful," the woman behind us with a Wisconsin Badgers t-shirt says. "such expressive colors."

"It really is quaint down here, isn't it?" her husband answers.

"Can you imagine what it would be like to live here?" she says.

"Oh, God, no." He's horrified. "It's just pretty paint, Linda. Do you realize what the murder rate is here?"

∽

When we get back to Felicity Street the crowd has thankfully thinned, and it's just the regulars, murmuring and minding our business. Mack's still at work so I invite Mumps to our room and show him my personal piece from Ra. He looks impressed. I break him off a little.

"Our little secret," I say.

∽

X

We're all sitting around, itching. The histamines have been released, we scratch like we're allergic to pollen and the living room is springtime.

Mack's belly feels pregnant pressed against my back, his arms wrapped around me. In his lap, I am an egg in a basket. He asks me for a back scratch.

"Like a cat?" I ask.

"Just like a cat, baby."

❧

Mack loves watching me eat. Eggs Benedict with Andouille, baklava dripping with honey, slabs of bacon and alligator cheesecake. He especially loves to see me sop up sauce with chunks of bread. The first time he came on to me I was eating a Greek salad with my fingers. Sometimes at work, Mack will make me something special—elaborate sandwiches with roast beef and gruyere and multiple layers of toasted bread with fresh pesto, or crusty baked brie with apples and onion.

For the next two days, the Moonlight is closed because there's a movie filming on Sophie B. Wright Place. So tonight we're having dinner at home.

I am petitioning for spinach salad with raspberries and almonds (not pecans) and a lot of goat cheese. Mack says, whatever I want, I'm his baby, as long as I eat it with my fingers. He doesn't care about the salad, anyway. He leaves the house, on a tarragon mission, he says. As he walks out the door, he kisses me long and special, and tells me I'm the prettiest thing he's ever seen.

∾

I should be grateful Ra's product has been so good lately. Weird, though, because it's not that I've been nodding longer, or harder, just that I've been scritching more.

∾

At the Sack 'n Save, there is a woman in front of me buying cat food and Hormel Chili. I imagine her with a tail.

My purse is heavy with the slip-slip-slip of goat cheese and a bag of spinach, a carton of raspberries, a paper-wrapped package of steak, and Pinwheel cookies. The woman with the tail counts out exact change as I shift my weight, scratch my scalp. Penny, penny, penny, come on. I put sponge cake, a bottle of table wine, and a yam on the conveyor belt.

"This all for you today?" The lady behind the register has mismatched thumbs.

Mumps waits for me in the parking lot. I open the Pinwheels in the car and we eat half the package before we get back to the house.

"You wanna stay for dinner," I ask.

"Just a shot," Mumps says, "I have to get home to Grace. She's making meatloaf."

"Gross."

"Just because you had a mother who shunned the tried and true American recipes of the era doesn't mean the rest of us are gross," he says.

"It's just the name," I say, "loaf." Goddamnit, right behind my ear, so fucking itchy.

Chip is in a horrible mood when we get inside with the food. The microwave is making popping noises, shooting bursts of light every few seconds.

"Chip, what's going on in here?" I press the end button.

Chip is doing his moon-man walk, all slow and bent at the knees. Chip's knees always seem bent—I fear for his joints. "What'd you do that for," he snaps.

Mumps jumps in to defend me. "The microwave was about to explode," he says.

"Ship fulla fools," Chip mutters as he pops open the microwave door, bends even lower and sticks his head practically inside the box. He pulls out a plate of cocaine becoming crack and hurries back to his room making little huffing noises to let us know the plate is hot to touch. "I'm gonna have to get with Vern tonight, now," he calls back to us.

"Drama queen," I say to Mumps. I scratch my neck.

We go to my room where Mack reads *Harper's Index*.

"Did you know that a minimum of 4000 people have registered to vote in strip clubs since 2003?" he asks without looking up from the magazine.

"Illuminating," I say. "We're going to get down real quick."

"Yeah," he says, "I didn't even know you could register to vote in a strip club. You'd think the puritans would have some statute against it. Did you get the groceries?"

"Whenever you want to start cooking, I'm starving. Did you find tarragon?"

"Mission complete. The only woman to win the Miss America pageant twice weighed 140 pounds. How much do you weigh, baby? Gotta be less than that, huh?"

"That's rude," Mumps says.

Mack looks up from his magazine. "What?" he asks. "Claire could be Miss America is all I'm saying."

∽

I almost burnt the kitchen down last time I made a grilled cheese sandwich. I exclusively date men who can make good sauce. Mack's specialty is béarnaise, which is excellent on steak. Also quite delicious on pork, which is what Mack prefers. I'm a beef girl myself, and since I'm the one who goes to the grocery store, I feel the executive decisions are mine.

"This isn't going to feed five people," Mack says from the kitchen.

I have found red and have to keep concentrating on the remainder of steps needed to finish this shot. Push, press, pull, release.

"There's only four of us," I say to my arm, "Mumps has other plans."

∽

"My girlfriend is the best girlfriend in the world, my pretty girlfriend is the best girl in the world. Oh, my girlfriend is the best girl in the world. I love her all day long." Mack sings in the kitchen as he whisks eggs.

I sit in the bedroom, smiling, drenching bits of toilet paper in nail polish remover and making my toes tiny blank slates.

I hear Jennifer ring the bell on her bike basket as she pulls up. She brings bread and more wine. I don't know why we're all buying wine as if we give a shit about drinking.

Chip, Jennifer and I cook shots and get down as the sauce reduces. Mack asks me if I can watch the stove while he gets his turn, and I'm nervous because I might ruin our night. As he leaves the kitchen, he turns around and winks.

"Baby, even if you burned the sauce, I'd still love you."

∽

Chip makes coffee after dinner, which seems redundant given the crack we smoke as the food digests.

But I have a cup. And Jennifer has a cup. Mack doesn't drink coffee because it stains your teeth.

∽

I'm washing dishes in the kitchen and a roach flies for my head—I think they must have magnets, they always go straight for the head. I scream and Mack comes in.

"Roach," I say. It has landed on the counter, by the sink. "Get me a shoe."

Mack takes off his sneaker and hands it to me. I slam it on the roach, twice, because I heard on Animal Planet that roaches have two brains—one in their head and one in their ass. I smash it one more time, its wings still fluttering.

"It's dead already," Mack says. "You don't have to demolish it completely. You aren't scared of little bugs are you?"

He takes the shoe from me and uses it to brush the smashed body off the counter and into the trashcan.

"It's perfectly normal to be afraid of bugs. They eat us when we die."

❧

Calorie Count for the Day:

> 7 Pinwheel Cookies- 840
> Béarnaise Sauce- 260
> Steak- 180
> French Bread- 150
> Sweet Potatoes- 130
> Almonds- 80
> Goat Cheese- 76
> Butter- 36
> Whole Milk- 30
> Raspberries- 16
> Spinach-7
> Coffee- 7

❧

"I've been really itchy lately," I say as we're watching the news after dinner.

"That's cause we keep you in such good medicine," Chip laughs. "That's one of the warning signs," he says in a made-for-TV-movie voice. "Dilated pupils, lethargy, slowed speech patterns, itchiness, lack of concentration, constipation," he peters out, closing his eyes for a moment. Opens them quick like, real wide, "You constipated, Claire?"

I look at Mack. "I don't know," I say. "It's really fucking itchy. Are you itchy?"

"Only when I'm high," Mack says. "Chip's right. You get taken care of better than any of us."

Dan Rather plays a clip of Dick Cheney explaining we need a surge.

"Don't complain," Mack says.

"She's just grumpy because she's constipated," Chip says.

I blush.

Mack shakes his head at the news and goes back to our room. The numbers on the VCR switch from 10:59 to 11:00, and Jennifer leaves for work on her bike, leftover sponge cake in the basket.

Jennifer works at Molly's at the Market. She works the back bar, which is the better bar to work since most of the tourists who come in off Decatur don't realize it's there. Jennifer took the job when Chip heard Erica got fired.

There are certain instances when Chip's hennish qualities work in our favor.

∾

Erica is Mack's ex-girlfriend. She has a new boyfriend, Vern. Vern lives in the neighborhood, too. He comes around sometimes. He and Chip have an arrangement. If Vern or Chip run out before Ra can re-up, they depend on each other. Sometimes I go to Vern's with Chip if I'm bored.

Mack never goes because he might run into Erica. Erica gave Mack herpes. He says it's dormant and I've never seen a sore, so I believe him.

Erica is tall and Asian and from the West Bank. She's also adopted, and used to be a ballerina. She and Mack met when she worked at the Moonlight. When they broke up, she went to work at Molly's, and now she just goes on dates. Mack hates her. I wonder if he will hate me. At least I didn't give him herpes.

When Jennifer leaves on her bike, Chip asks me if I want to take a walk down to Vern's.

∾

Things on the coffee table at Vern's:
    4 watches of varying quality
    2 vases, daisies
    1 stack *Vibe* magazines

9 opened rolls of Lifesavers
3 Phillies Blunts, unopened
1 tube lipstick
1 digital scale
1 apple cinnamon candle
1 bottle Tums
1 box set Ally McBeal videotapes
1 box Ziploc Baggies
10 single Kool 100's
1 package Lee press-on nails

∽

My neck itches.

∽

"How much you take for this watch?" Chip asks, picking up a heavy, silver Rolex knock-off.

Vern takes it from Chip, inspects it, switching from hand to hand, testing the clasp. "Twenty bucks."

"I'll give you ten."

"Sold to the man from Felicity Street," Vern says. "How's the operation over there?"

"Rolling along until this ding-dong went and turned off the microwave this afternoon." Chip pretends to put his hands around my neck and wring. "How much hard you think you can spare?"

"Gram or two, that's all. Ra ain't been answerin' the phone since this morning."

"I know. Told me he had to take his lady to the movies tonight."

"Ah, alright then, he's back up tomorrow." Vern nods his head, relieved.

"Oh, yeah, gotta keep the ladies happy." Chip rubs my shoulder.

"Don't I know that," Vern looks at Erica, who is lying on the couch, bare feet hung over the fuzzy green armrest. "Don't I know it."

"Two grams, then," Chip says, and they go into the other room.

Erica and I are in the living room alone, her feet rocking back and forth gently. She points her toes, flexes, points and flexes. I scratch behind my ears.

"You still with Mack?" she asks me.

"Yeah," I say, "he's back at the house."

"You tell him he doesn't have to be scared to come around here, I'm not rabid."

I fake-laugh.

She continues, "It's not like I'm gonna start a fight or something. We're both happy now. Vern's so good to me, I'm really, really lucky."

I fake-laugh again, even though I don't think she was being funny.

"He still dormant?" she asks.

I fake-laugh. And then I realize I've been asked a direct question which pertains to my vagina. "Oh, oh, yes."

Chip and Vern come back in the room, I exhale finally.

"What about this?" Chip picks up an old Earth, Wind and Fire record, "This for sale?"

"Man, don't you know everything in this house is for sale," Vern lets out a long laugh.

I look at Erica. She smiles as Vern picks up her outstretched legs and sits down underneath them.

We get back to the house and my head will not stop itching. I know what dope feels like and it doesn't feel like this. Mack is asleep and the radio is on. Zephyrs tickets are $2. Airport Freeway is closed due to construction, use River Road. Mayor Nagin will hold a town hall meeting at the Martin Luther King Jr. Community Center. Now back to Art Bell.

I try the pillow beside Mack, kiss his head a few times, think about Erica, get back up and scratch for a few moments, see what Chip is up to.

∾

Chip is smoking in his bedroom, rolling the glass pipe around in his fingers, warming it then lighting the piece, hold, bells ring in his head, I can almost hear them through his skull.

"You want this?" he asks.

I hear bells ring in my own ears and wonder why anyone ever takes the next hit when the first one has all the music.

∾

Wet from the shower, I am inspecting the back of my ears and neck in the mirror. Fuck.

∾

Nix costs fucking $19.99 at the Walgreens. If there's anything to go brand name on, it's lice shampoo. The back of the box advises me not to use the shampoo around or in my vagina.

∾

There is a vacuum sealer at the Moonlight for portioning and freezing. I bring the pillows and couch cushions to my shift, press plastic around them and seal. Chip picks them up and hides them in the closet. I keep my hair in a hive at the top of my head, make sure to hold my head up as I shake the tumbler.

∾

"It's from that fucking couch at The Saint," Mack says, "I told you that place is dirty."

"You can't get lice from sitting on a couch," I say. My head is burning, dark red shampoo staining my hairline, blood halo. I sit on our stripped bed, keeping still even though I want to shake my hair all over him. "You're going to have to shave your head," I say.

"Fuck that. You're the one with all the hair."

"No one wants me to shave my head," I say, "I don't have the jawline for it."

∾

The head louse:
 Spends its entire life on a human scalp
 Feeds exclusively on human blood
 Lives for approximately one month

∾

When we cut open the seals, dead bits of gray fall to the seams of the bag like dandruff. Mumps drives me to the car wash to vacuum the pillows and cushions. We throw the plastic wrap in the dumpster behind Zara's Grocery and I shiver a little bit. You can see their tiny claws.

∾

There are living things breeding in my head, fucking and sucking and eating and laying eggs, they're being born and dying on my head.

I read Anne Frank too young, 7 or 8, I must have been. I was convinced the Nazis were planning a surprise attack on America and since I was the only one aware of this, they would come for my family first. This led to elaborate precautionary measures. I needed to be with an adult, able-bodied woman at all times—one who would be sent to the work line and not the death line. I located spaces large enough for a family to hide, the first being the AV room at Our Lady of Perpetual Hope Elementary School. Smaller places I could hide alone. The massive organ pipes at the Meyerson Symphony Center. The cabinet beneath the school stage where the folding chairs were stored.

But the worst part was the nightmares:
> The Nazis find my family hiding in the AV room
> We are evacuated from Dallas on the train tracks that run through Casa Linda Park
> We arrive at a camp and I hide underneath my mother's peasant skirt
> We are in the showers, naked
> A woman stands over my head with an electric shaver

And then I woke up—always right before my hair was shaved.

∾

The teeth of the bright blue comb feel incredible against my scalp. Each spike digs into my skin. I start at the top of my hairline and stop at the nape of my neck. Then I repeat starting at the neck, down to the tips of my split ends. Each time checking for living lice. The ones that are still crawling on the comb are the worst. I drop them in the toilet until there are about a dozen, flush. I do this for two hours.

My mother and I fought every morning as she brushed my hair before school, I would cry every morning.

The nurse at Our Lady of Perpetual Hope pulled our hair up hard from the neck, from the hairline, for piojos check every quarter. Everyone knew who had piojos because you didn't come back from the nurse's office. My sister and I were sent home one year. They gave you a green slip of paper with extermination instructions and a box of generic lice shampoo.

Our mother took the barstools from the kitchen to the porch, made us comb each other's heads outside as she stripped the house and filled the laundry room with overflowing baskets. She went to the store for Clorox and told us to start all over and not to come back inside for any reason. She brought a pitcher of Crystal Light and set it outside the French doors.

My sister is in the first year of her residency at Baylor. She's going to be a dermatologist.

∾

When Mack comes home I am nodding a little, but the comb is in my hand, stuck at the top of my forehead. There was a thought there, in my scalp, about Our Lady of Perpetual Hope, but I lost it.

"Jesus Christ," he says, shaking my shoulders. "Get it together. You can't nod at a time like this."

He leaves the room and I hear him bitching to Chip.

Fuck him.

I inspect the blue teeth, they are stacked with white dots and grey bodies. There is one crawling toward the handle. I pinch it and it bleeds all over my finger like a mosquito. I throw the comb in the opened Nix box. I toss it all into the Zara's dumpster, stop at Walgreens again before the laundromat.

∾

I blow on my coffee as I wait for the dryers to buzz. Mack says he spends half his life waiting. I will wait nine days for the eggs laid today to hatch.

∾

Lice:
    Cannot jump or fly, but have been known to be carried in the wind

Bite the scalp 4-5 times daily to feed
Live and breed best in warm climates

∽

At work, I can't help squeezing the root of each hair between my thumb and finger. Some eggs are big enough I can throw them in the sink where I wash the glasses.

∽

I go to the Marigny to escape another lecture about my beautiful hair. Chico is playing drums for a show at The Spotted Cat. I drink whiskey sours with Mento, Chico's bass player, and tell him about the bugs in my head.

"Black people don't get lice," he tells me, smiling. "You can still sleep over at my house anytime you want, Claire."

After the show, Mento tells Chico, who grimaces. White kids are stupid, how did I get so stupid, stupid gringo girl. We go to Mento's house. Chico confirms that Mento's head is safe, but his house is off limits until the piojos are all dead, all the way.

Lice is the only word I actually think of in Spanish.

∽

Mating habits of the adult head louse:
Mating begins within the first 10 hours of adult life
Copulation can last longer than an hour

Adult lice will copulate up to five times a day and twice that at night

Adult females die during intercourse, having laid approximately 150 eggs

∾

When I get back to Felicity Street it is late and Mack is sleeping on the sheets, crisp and smelling like "Spring Fresh Breeze." His head is smooth and slick and I cup it in my hands as I crawl under the leopard print blanket. It feels soft against my cheek, moisturized, new. I kiss the back of his neck, with its tiny rising bumps, wake him up with my teeth pulling at his earlobes.

"I'm sorry I yelled at you," he says, words half-caught in his sleeping throat.

"It's okay, baby," I kiss his shoulders, "I love you."

"I love you, too," he says, "I love you even with bugs." He squeezes my fat. "I love your bugs and your fat and your—"

"It's okay," I say. "We don't have to go through the list."

∾

It is disgusting to eat, because I can only think of how my bugs eat. On me. It is their feeding that creates the itching sensation. They slam their fangs into my scalp, they secrete saliva that prevents blood clots. As long as they're feeding, they're also shitting, so my head is full of bug feces.

∾

It seems unfair that the bugs always find red while I have to search for a line that will hit. That bugs shit as long as they eat, while I am always constipated. Bugs don't pay rent. Bugs only live for a month, fucking and eating and shitting and living rent-free, and then they get to die wherever they are, usually clamped to the legs of another bug fucking them. If I only had to live for a month, things would be different.

Mack and I put on our sunglasses and walk to Sophie's Creamery for breakfast.

"Don't walk on the outside," Mack says. He switches places with me on the sidewalk.

I remember something from 5th grade etiquette class about men walking nearer to traffic. Something about sludge and grime sloshing on a lady's fine dress.

But he continues, "You're not for sale."

I lean my shoulder into him, hold his hand.

XI

"What is it?" I ask. "Oh god, I think it's a mouse—a rat, something, oh." We are circling Bayou St. John, meeting Suzette on Ponce De Leon by the racetrack.

"That's just a baby squirrel," Chip says, "too small to be a rat."

❧

Warring died on the couch Tuesday as we smoked crack in the living room. He'd told his sister from Iowa to leave him be, even though she wanted to hire a hospice nurse. Why be doled out bits of morphine when you can get the real thing?

We took turns rubbing ice chips along the corners of his mouth and holding the glass pipe to his chappy lips. Every hour, Jennifer would cook a get-right for him, on the house.

Most people had heard to stay away from our place since there was an old dude dying on the couch, but there were people who didn't know or didn't care, and when they came over Chip told them the shop was closed, family emergency, he said.

❧

Suzette wears a lemon housedress and bright blue gym shorts. You can see the shorts through the dress, they are big, like they are made for a man. "I thought you were taking me for oysters," she says.

"I told you a million times, Ma, we're taking you to the Rite-Aid," Chip says.

Suzette is behind us, and Chip looks over his shoulder every few steps to make sure she hasn't bolted. The thing I hate most about Suzette is the way she says my name. At the end, lay-uh. Like I'm covered in layers. Cuh-lay-uh. God, I hate that.

"You got your ID, Ma?"

Chip takes steps so big I could lay down in the stride. Suzette stops and forages through her purse, dropping little bits of Kleenex and Werther's candy wrappers. She holds her driver's license above her head and makes some wooting sounds.

Suzette isn't related to Warring, but they have the same last name—Herbert. Chip's got a different last name—his father's, Terrebonne, not the one we need for picking up Warring's leftover prescriptions.

∾

At Rite-Aid I have:
    Listened to Suzette tell the pharmacist her husband's
    too sick to leave the house
    Looked through the greeting cards
    Opened a box of Triscuits, eaten several and returned
    the box to the shelf
    Tested various shades of lipstick
    Given Suzette bus fare, twice
    Purchased a bag of Swedish Fish
    Gone outside to smoke a cigarette
    Left without a goodbye. This is a ridiculous wait.

∾

I don't know what bus to take from Mid-City to the Marigny, so I walk down Esplanade toward Chico's. I have been visiting Chico more often than usual, though not as often as I visited before I moved to Felicity Street.

Chico calls me skinny and feeds me chorizo and makes me avocado, banana and honey smoothies. He says they will put the right kind of fat on me. You need some fucking vitamin, he says. Chico still gets his plurals and genders switched sometimes, other times he sounds like a grammar book. If you can swing between two worlds like that, you'd be a fool not to do it.

∾

Chico knows how to run numbers, like my dad. My dad didn't teach me much, but he did teach me numbers, how to make a profit, figure in the bottom line, weigh risk and reward. What's the greatest potential profit from the least possible risk? Go and get that. And I do. I am a for-profit operation. That's why Hassan trusts me at the Moonlight. I'll tell him when we're wasting money keeping the lights on, he knows I'll start the $1 special a little late and end it a little early, that I pour a little short on the fruity drinks, a little stiff for the neats and rocks—let people think they're getting a great deal.

Thinking about the Moonlight makes me queasy, though. I focus on the live oaks and the cypresses, make two columns in my head and tally them as I walk down to the Marigny.

∾

When I think this city is going to make me permanently sick, something reminds me that I live in the livingest place ever. There's forty or so of them, a neighborhood parade bringing out their dead, and I wish we knew musicians, so we could blow a horn for Warring. How we could dip and thump and clap and shake. We could wear white and strangers would join in, because they would know by the way we moved that Warring was a man who lived. This is the real jazz.

∾

Chico's house is temperature cool, even though he lives on the third floor. The windows are open; there is plant life. Butcher paper used to cover the card table, and I'd bring crayons over and color tablecloths. Now he has a butcher block, no paper. He wedges knives along the edge closest to the wall.

The kitchen is hot, though. He's cooking cow tongue, lengua, which I will not eat.

Chico slaps the back of me, "You skinnyass, you skinnyass gringo girl," he says.

All my life I have wanted to be called skinny as if it were an insult. He pulls the waistband up on my jeans, I hop a little, and he hands me a joint.

Chico reminds me of a cactus, short and roundish, mostly bald, but with prickly hairs poking here and there from the sides of his head, and the way he winks makes me think there's always a juicy secret on the inside.

"My babies are blooming," he says, "you fire that, skinnygirl." I struggle to light it, sticky. Chico checks the tongue. "We need some more peppers," he calls back.

Spilling from the screened-in porch are hibiscus and mint, succulents and snapdragons, sage, rosemary and three kinds of basil, even a bird of paradise, a pineapple plant, lemon trees that Chico says he'll transfer to the yard soon. In all that plant life, there are no peppers growing.

We go to the Verdi Mart even though they do not sell peppers. There will be people there and food to eat, and since we don't have peppers for the cow tongue, the lengua is ruined--without peppers it's bland as grass—we'll eat macaroni and cheese instead.

❦

Tattoos I see at the Verdi Mart:
    Portrait of Abraham Lincoln
    Dragon eating a snake eating a mouse
    Crucifix made of rifles
    504
    Cricket
    Trombone
    Portrait of Huey P. Long
    Dunce cap
    Oil lamp

❦

I don't go home before work. Suzette is sitting on our couch and will sit there for several more days. This is another thing I hate about Suzette.

I bring the leftover macaroni and cheese to my Moonlight shift, cover it in A-1 and eat from the Styrofoam box. Steve-D looks disgusted.

I'm not going home when I get out of this shift, tomorrow mid-morning. Respectable places will be open for business. I patronize respectable businesses in daylight hours.

❦

Mumps doesn't even sit down, just leans over the bar and palms the Discover into my hand.

"What do you have?" he asks.

"Whatever you want, look at this fucking zoo."

"Well run me two-fifty then. You want me to put an order into Chip for you? I'll bring it back for your trouble."

"I guess order me a ten-pack, if it's not too much trouble."

I run the card and hand over the cash.

"Thanks, Mumps, you're the best."

"See you in a few," he says, and for once, he doesn't look uncomfortable, pushing his way through the crowd. His shoulders look filled out and almost handsome.

I am at the Rose Café, patronizing respectable businesses. Daylight. Waiting for Chico and Mento, and why they aren't here I don't know. I thought they were always here.

I am sitting catty-corner of two women. They have tattoos, slightly out-of-date hipness. One has asymmetrical bangs, the other a fedora. I may have seen the one with bangs somewhere. They're everywhere, those bangs. Goofy, I think.

"So they want me to make this list," the one with bangs says, "talking about what my triggers are, like I have triggers." Her voice sounds like there's a rock stuck in her nose. It's possible.

"Everyone has triggers," says Fedora.

"In that case, I'd say skin. That's mine. Skin." She blows on her foam, the long side of her bangs dip in. Fedora takes the fedora off and leans over. About to impart wisdom, she shakes the hair from her face and she has a lazy eye and a huge scar stretching across her left cheek.

"Wear long sleeves, then," she says.

That's all she's got, I guess.

The one with bangs looks up from the foam. "Those remind me of using, too," she says. "The way everyone has to wear long sleeves in August."

I see Chico turning the corner on Lafayette. He is wearing a muscle shirt and gray sweatpants cut off slightly below the knee, plastic sandals and a satchel around his neck that looks like what my grandmother puts in her underwear drawer. Mento walks his bike. I leave my bubble tea on the table, meet them mid-way.

"Whatever happened to anyone being just pretty?" I ask.

～

Mumps is on the couch when I get to Felicity Street. Other people are on the couch, too, including Suzette. Chip is bent at the knees, his eyes closed and Mack is in the bedroom, paging through mid-90s porn no doubt. I press a bill into Mumps' chest.

"Thanks for the delivery service," I say. "You're a doll."

"No, you're a doll, Claire," Mumps says, beautiful standard American English. "This is too much, though. I owe you twenty."

"You don't."

Mumps presses a twenty into my hand. I add it to the Boulder envelope. It's getting thick.

∾

The Femoral Artery:
>   Ends just above the knee at the Adductor Canal, known commonly as Hunter's Canal
>   Provides blood to the thigh, knee and foot through deep and superficial routes
>   Can be used to draw blood when blood pressure is so low that radial arteries disappear

∾

"Chip, baby, Chip."

"What, ma?"

"Chip. Chip. Chip."

"Ma!"

"Chip. Where those Herbert pills?"

"Right where you left—"

"Chip, don't yell at me, baby, baby, don't yell so much."

I wish I could trade Suzette to have Warring back. A Herbert for a Herbert. Surely no one would notice.

∾

Mack is so fucking predictable in his porn, political satire, drugs and soup. Things he finds insufferable: pop music, young mothers and college kids. He does not vary from his schedule, which includes all the things he enjoys, plus work. He also enjoys blowjobs. That is what I am here for. I am also here to learn about political satire, and politics in general. He forgives that I was recently in college. I still read even though I am not earning grades. Mack respects reading.

∾

This will go on all night. I keep the radio tuned to AM talk when I cannot sleep. Mack likes it, too.

Something about dredging and sediment, about public hearings and erosion and coastal protection plans. Something about acts of Congress and tax dollars and pumping.

❧

I wake up and the talk has turned to sports. Off. I make the bed. Making the bed sets the tone for your day. Mack is gone. Suzette sleeps on the couch, her yellow dress scrunched up above the gym shorts.

❧

When Ra leaves, Chip and I run a test and do the numbers. The test results are so good and so strong I have trouble keeping the 2:1 and the 3:1 envelopes straight.

❧

"I'll get you back, Claire."

"Not a big deal, Mumps. Seriously. Happy to help."

"But, I will. You're a lifesaver."

It's a love letter in a foil envelope. I sit criss-cross apple-sauce on the floor looking up at him perched on the bed, lumpy cat. Of all the people who lean and lie on my bed, I like Mumps best. I have never seen his cock, which makes it easier.

He finds a line quick because he has boy arms that pop blue. I am having trouble with my arms, looking for one in my thigh. Mumps is counting. 14, 15—

❧

He does not make it to 26.

❧

"What the fuck?" Chip is not pleased.

"What the fuck, what? I just gave him a shot."

"You give him the motherfucking batch we just made for us? That's for us. You get that? We're used to that. We're the ones doing that shit every day, he's not used to that. Goddamnit. What are you going to do with this?"

"What do you mean what am I going to do with this?" I am confused. This is not a this. This is a body, a person, Mumps.

"All I know is you better stop crying and get to gettin' on this shit. People gonna be over here before you know it and there can't be this here."

"Chip," I say, real quiet, like a little girl, "look,"—and I show him my thigh, with the silver steel tip pushed almost all the way in. "He fell on me."

"Shit. Okay. Come on. You're gonna need some tweezers, but we'll get to that in a minute."

We hear the door, and Chip's eyes open so wide I think the balls are gonna pop right out of their sockets. I don't know what to do besides hide in the bathtub and pull the shower curtain like hide-and-seek.

It's just Mack.

"She gave him the good shit," I hear Chip panting. My face is raining and I can taste the sweetness from my nose dripping onto my lips.

"Come on. Come on." I can feel Chip's hands on my shoulders, pulling me out of the bathtub, steering me, pushing me over the sink, turning the knobs, letting the water rush over my hair. "You gotta calm down now, girl, this is gonna happen."

I push my head up from the water. "What's gonna happen?"

"This mess is gonna get out of our house. Clean-up's gonna happen."

Mack holds my hair back like I'm throwing up. "I'm gonna help you, baby," he says. "Don't worry, everything's gonna be alright, everything's fine. We've got to get that needle out of your leg, okay, baby, okay? We've got to clean up and get him out of here so we can make sure you're alright."

We carry Mumps to his car. Drag him, really—he's heavy. He parked in the alley, but once we get him there we realize the car's locked and we don't have the keys. They must have fallen out of his pocket, so I go back to my room and see them, WWOZ keychain and his wallet, too.

It pays to Discover. I wonder how long it will take his parents to cancel the card. They'll probably be too grief-stricken to do it immediately. I am a bad person. My leg throbs.

Chip is back.

"Come on! What'cha doin' in here," then he looks down at the wallet and he sees what I see, "Gimme that," and he pulls the card out of the wallet, shoves it into his pocket and goes back to the alley.

We put Mumps in the back seat, me holding his head in my lap, Mack and Chip in the front. Chip says we need to drive the car someplace else, someplace public. We go to Walgreens since I need tweezers to get the needle out of my leg. Chip and Mack go in and I wait in the car with Mumps. He has changed colors a couple of times since he fell. Reddy pink, and then grey, and now blue.

My mind has to be protecting me by jumping to Violet Beauregarde. He looks heavier than usual, his stomach all slung to one side. I remember making guacamole on his porch, back on Oak Street, him scraping the metal bowl with his fat fingers, getting every last speck of cilantro and onion.

They come back with tweezers, a pint of Rocky Road and two Diet Dr. Peppers.

"This'll make you feel better, baby," Mack says, and hands me the ice cream.

"Where are we going to go?" I ask.

"This'll do," Chip says, "this is plenty public."

෴

I swear I can feel bones stacking on top of me.

෴

XII

Enough already. I have to stop thinking about:
Fingerprints
Blueberries
Pawn shops
Incinerators
Price tags dangling off my limbs
Being marked down
That bottle of bleach underneath the sink
Drowning

Mack knows what he's doing, leaving notes in the morning and offering me the first shot off every bag. He keeps telling me to let it go, we all make choices, it could have been any one of us, he even pretends that he liked Mumps.

But I turn down every first shot and I throw the notes away before I read the second word, and whenever he says something about choices, I just go to the kitchen and stare into the refrigerator and shake the milk carton again.

Chico tells me about his daughter, Layla, who lives in Santa Cruz. And he tells me about his ex-wife, who he never lived on the same side of their duplex with.

"Some people you never need to live with," he says, happy about it. "You, too."

"I know," I say, "I'm so fucking hard to live with."

"Shut up, stupid. You feeling so stupid sorry for yourself. It's a good thing you should be alone."

He means it as a compliment, but he's going to die alone, in a house full of illegal plant matter and who knows if his daughter will ever even know.

"You know what you need to do?" he asks.

"I've got to get clean," I say.

"No big deal," he says, stringing it all together like one word. "Not so hard. What you need to do is take a cold shower and stick a thumb up your ass, stop the shriveling."

"I think you mean sniveling."

"I know what I mean."

"Did you ever live with Layla?" I ask.

"Go do something," he says. "Go do something by yourself and find some cold water, go get tough."

∾

The kids at the Moon Rocks let their dogs wade in the water, their long paw nails getting caught in the green fencing on top of the boulders stacked along the banks. There are so many of them here this time of year, when the weather in Seattle and Portland and Chicago and New York is still too cold to sleep outside. They come for Mardi Gras and stay through Jazz Fest, just like the others. I give them credit for saving money on hotel rooms. That, they're smart about. I wonder what it would be like to go, just go, the way they do, to the next warm place to sleep outside. I wonder, is it an admirable quality to be incapable of living with other people.

∾

In the dreams, the drowning starts slowly—a single drip. Then drip drip. Builds until I am staring up at the sky like a chicken, throat full of water, gurgle, gurgle, die.

∾

Every time Mack puts his arm around me, I cringe. I ask him what he would do with my body, with my wallet, with my phone, if he would even look up my mother's number.

You don't even like your mother, he says. And besides, I would never let that happen to you, baby.

I believe him a little less every time he says it, and every time, I swallow another stitch of silence and stack those stitches like armor inside me.

~

If the police don't come, then Mumps' parents will call, and if his parents don't call, Grace will figure it out, and if Grace doesn't figure it out, the Discover people will, and if the Discover people don't figure it out, then Chip will keep buying bushels of expensive shrimp and I will never be able to eat again.

I look in the back pocket of my jeans, but no envelope. I look between the tank tops and bras and old bent outfits. At the back of the drawer, crumpled into a ball, is my envelope, everything gone. I wonder, does Mack think I wouldn't just lend him the money if he asked. Does he actually think there's anything I can say no to?

I've got to find a way to save money.

~

Ra is in Chip's room.

"Where's this girl been?" Ra asks, even though he is really asking me, I'm this girl.

"I'm off today," I answer. "I must've needed the sleep."

I smile.

"Been waitin'," he says. "Your man at work?"

Ra smiles back.

"Chip here wants to place an order, you want to help him out?" He is missing a tooth near the back of his mouth, and when he smiles, there's a gap at the corners. I can see the hole. I wonder why he doesn't fill it in with gold.

I have my teeth, all originals. I have a pretty smile for anyone, not just in comparison to people without teeth.

We go back to the bedroom and I am glad I made the bed.

Ra's belt is heavy, a Gucci copy from the French market, five dollars, but still durable, with one of those square buckles I'm not sure how to work. I'm grateful he unfastens it himself. And sits. Reclines. Rests his head on a peach pillowcase—I get the jersey sheets, the ones Oprah likes. Oprah doesn't lie, they're like sleeping on a well-washed t-shirt.

Ra's wearing stiff dark jeans, his underwear are Calvin Klein, boxer briefs. White. He doesn't take either all the way off, but leaves them drooping around his knees. I'm not sure if he wants me to pull them all the way down or if this is a signal to be expedient. He acts like this has happened before.

I choose brevity.

Ra makes some humming noises. I sneak my eyes up, try to gauge my performance, his eyes are closed, mouth wide open, there is another missing tooth I hadn't noticed before. I think about the kindergartner I used to tutor in San Antonio who had a complete set of silver baby teeth.

There.

∽

"You musta done him good, cause this shit tastes close to raw." Chip licks his finger and winces bitter.

∽

I brush my teeth and try not to think too much about the bleach underneath the sink. I can feel it pressing against my palm, the dusty cap. I know the cap is dusty because I have gotten close, it wouldn't taste any worse than Everclear. I try to get in and out of the bathroom like those no-fix, no-tricks rules apply to me, because I can feel the smooth curve of that bottle fit into the smoother curve of my palm.

∽

We repeat the same things every day.

We make the same walk down Felicity, over to Josephine, up Camp, there's Magazine, there's Esplanade, there's Rampart. We don't go that far, the streets are in the back of our minds, ready for us if we did keep walking. Same gestures, phrases spoken at each other, we pretend they constitute conversation. It's just acknowledgment that the transaction has been made, that we will make it again tomorrow.

And it's not we. It's me. I'm in that room with Ra, I'm behind the bar alone, I'm on the bus. It's strange how alone I can feel with a dick in my mouth. Sometimes it feels so much a part of me I think I'm pregnant with it, pregnant with the dick and with the dope, but then I remember, no, alone. If I was smart, I would latch onto that thing inside me, make it let me feel not so lonely.

∾

Things I am almost certain Chip has purchased with the Discover:

    Juicer
    Digital scale
    Bright blue jogging suit that crinkles when he walks
    Screw gun
    Disposable cameras
    A frozen box of hamburger patties
    Gold Toe Socks
    Rubber tubing
    Karaoke machine
    God, all those shrimp

∾

Mack and I no longer speak. We speak to each other, if we happen to be in the same room at the same time, in the presence of other people who are talking. But we do not say anything in bed. We don't fuck, we don't argue, we don't acknowledge that anything is wrong. Thank God we are junkies and not cokeheads, and it is natural for us to be silent and still and sleepy.

∽

Ra looks me up and down every day like he's never seen me before. There's no more winking. He still smiles, when it's over, when he gives me my private piece, and when he walks back into Chip's room, he smiles then. He should be smiling. He gets everything he wants.

Ra pays me in dope and I pay me in cash. Every time Ra gives me a private piece, I put $10 in my Boulder envelope, which I hide in a box of tampons now. Two more weeks of this work and I can leave. It's worth it, to leave.

∽

Chico takes me to the Voodoo Spiritual Temple on Rampart after I ask him for the tenth time. We walk in silence. Chico is like everyone else who doesn't have anything to say to me. When I ask Priestess Miriam for something to protect me from death she presses a sapphire-colored stone into my palm and charges me a buck for a brown glass bottle of oil. Chico shakes his head.

"If I knew you was coming for that, I could make you oil in my house."

"I need something real," I say.

"You don't need some oil to keep away death," he says.

"It can't hurt."

"I can't believe you spent a dollar," he says, "I thought you only spent dollars on dope."

"Not anymore," I say, and he looks at me squinty.

"And why that?"

∾

Ra asks me to come along on some runs. I sit in the passenger's seat and we're way above the potholes and squirrels with his giant Navigator and tires. He spreads his big palm across the back of my neck. He doesn't rub, just rests his hand there. I can't stop looking in the rearview and the side mirrors. Ra thinks it's funny I'm so scared.

∾

Chico's right, I don't need anything to ward off death. We ward off death with repetition. Morning and night are irrelevant, there's no sleep, just deep nods, weeks go by without the date ever changing, months. If we stay in that singular experience, we are all those other lost days further from death. The days stick to each other, and that gives the appearance of stillness, that we are not moving, that we are firm and solid in our refusal—but death may not be cooperating. I keep the WWOZ keychain and the St. Sebastian medal in my wallet, next to my ticket. Playing dead does not always mean death will not find you. I keep making the same motions regardless.

∾

Mumps' stupid idea about believing in something—I can't get this idea that I'm supposed to know some things for certain out of my head.

∾

Dead:
    Grandma Cunningham
    Grandpa Cunningham
    Grandpa Leland
    Hannah
    Bryan
    Shawn
    Shannon
    Emigdio
    Warring
    Mumps

It's just the grandparents who didn't die from dope.

∾

I play things between lines, I like the structure of boxes, I like being on a diet, like being with Ra, his hand pressed up against the back of my neck, steering me yes go there and get the fuck away from that. I think lists are like those lines, straight up and down, itemized inventory. Close in on a single piece of something.

The way Ra closes in on me. Ra makes me feel like a pit inside a peach—with his fuzzy little hairs q'ing all over him then me, pinning me to a body bigger than my own. That's what everybody wants—to be pinned to something bigger.

Other times, I swear, all I want is just ten minutes to walk under petals alone. Petal drop, petal drop. Make a movie of it, feet walking silent and petals. But a walk to work alone wouldn't mean I wasn't pinned—that's what those boys don't understand. They keep a finger pressed on me, when I won't go far.

Everybody all the way down to the Treme wants to get a piece of what Ra's got. Ra's the big middle. I'm lucky to be his look 'n see girl. All the way down to the Treme they want Ra, and what does Ra want? Me.

My mother said to me once, Why are you so afraid of having a normal life, you think it's gonna be boring? But the truth is, there's nothing more boring than a bang-it-in-my-arm every morning, nothing more routine than making the day into eight-hour boxes. I've made routine so fucking important I'm sick without it—on the floor, shitting sick.

∾

I know what every day looks like before it looks like a sun coming up. And that may not be beautiful, but I find order there.

Ra and I both do, and maybe that's why I keep sucking his dick. Maybe it's not for the money at all, because who am I kidding about moving to Boulder. I wouldn't move to Boulder if Ra bought me a first-class ticket tonight. Maybe I keep sucking his dick for the same reason he keeps coming for it. Ra and I, we know the danger of moving off this block. Where everyone is looking and seeing us. A thick white girl with Maybelline smeared on the backs of her elbows and a man with gaps in his mouth and so many kids he gets a discount on their fades. Where else except on this block would people give a shit about knowing our names?

So if I had to answer Mumps, I guess I believe in boxes. I believe in order.

❧

"You're all, all of you fucking women, you're all the fucking same."

"Enlightened."

"That's hilarious, Claire. You're enlightened? Is that what you're claiming right now? That you and your new-found prostitution are enlightened?"

"No, Mack. I'm just saying don't judge all womankind based on the few women you've dated."

"I've known enough."

"And you don't think you might be a common denominator there?"

"What are you trying to say? I make you do this shit? You're a big girl, Claire. I didn't make you do anything."

"I'm not saying that."

"I certainly didn't make you fuck some disgusting black drug dealer."

"Why's black coming into it?"

"Fucking Christ. You are so PC you can't even help it, you fucking liberal, coddled, integrity-impaired, adolescent, low self-esteem, suburbanite child."

"I'm not even from the suburbs! You're the one from the West Bank."

"Did it feel good, Claire? Did he have a big dick?"

"It stayed hard at least."

"I knew it. I knew you liked it. I knew you wanted it from the very first time you met him. I knew it."

"You know what, Mack? You're old."

XIII

When I left Felicity Street, Jennifer looked sad, like it was suddenly lonely in that place that's always full of people.

❧

Those rips inside me, the ones sewn up, those mystery stitches, I can feel them stacking taller on top of each other, pink and smooth on top of pink and smooth, over and over and over again.

❧

I swear, sometimes I want to rip inside him and feel the guts through my fingers. Break him apart like a block of ice with a pick, all slivers and chips. That's how much I love him. That's what it feels like. An ice pick in your guts.

❧

That's it, no more:
>   Stealing expensive cheese
>   Forgetting to wash my hands after I piss
>   Double punching the charge button on the credit card machine

Pinning a dollar bill to my shirt and pretending it's my
birthday
Going topless in the photo booth at The Saint

∾

Sleeping comfortably on a couch is a skill I have not yet mas-
tered. Chico's couch is a loveseat, Mento's couch is so old the
middle sinks. And it's a little difficult to ask a man to take
you back to his place and then insist you'd rather sleep on
the couch. But I pick up bartenders at last call, go home with
them, leave before they wake up, and then wind up wandering
around the Irish Channel until I have to be at the Moonlight.

∾

I can't sleep on Sydney Dobner's couch.

∾

I do a little spring cleaning at the Moonlight. The dust on
the ceiling fan is an inch thick—thick as the dust on the bottle of pisco, the top of that bleach bottle.

I pour myself a glass of the foggy brandy and add sour
mix, the best I can do. A pisco sour, like something Joan
Didion might drink on her balcony in Malibu. Mine must be
missing an ingredient, because it's disgusting.

The pullcord on the fan makes me think of strangling
something. Cleaning the mirrors doesn't help, either.

I take everything out of the coolers and shove my head
in, wipe down the stainless steel back of the box. I try to

keep my head in that cooler as long as I can stand it. I am the anti-Plath.

∾

Mack clocks in about an hour before I'll leave. We ignore each other and he deliberately loses the orders I punch in. I try to explain this to a man in a denim shirt that's been waiting on a pulled pork sandwich for forty-nine minutes.

∾

I call Chip when I leave the Moonlight. Mack won't be at Felicity Street, I need to get my stuff.

∾

The closet smells like chlorine and plastic and sulfur. Lining the back wall are my shoes, more carefully arranged than I have ever placed them, and I think for one second that Mack got sentimental and went through my things, needed to touch and smell them. And then I see: polka dot canvas flat, vintage Frye, red fuck-your-daddy pump, blue flip-flop, orange flip-flop, bright green Puma. All singular. All left. All thirteen pairs, right partner missing. When he knew I was in my dirty, black closed-toe work shoes. When he knows how much I hate those nursey Danskos.

∾

"Don't know a thing about it," Chip says, rummaging through a pile of laundry on the bedroom floor. "Now where is that damn thing?"

"What're you looking for?"

"Don't concern you."

"I was just trying to help."

"You get what you need?"

"Not really."

He looks up from the laundry, impatient and sharp.

"Well, what do you need from me?"

"I guess I don't need anything from you."

Chip pushes the pile to the wall with his bare foot, crawls on the floor to check under the bed.

"What'd you lose?" I ask again.

"Claire. You need something? Or you just want to pester me all night?"

He takes the cherrywood box off the bedside table and drops the contents on his comforter, and I see the Discover underneath a Ziploc bag of school photos, a freckled girl with a slight overbite, hair the color of mine. He picks up the bag and finds the card and sees me eyeing it.

"You think I was gonna cut it up? Finders keepers, girl."

"I didn't say anything."

"We know why you left."

❦

They don't know shit.

❦

Go to The Dragon's Den to spot Chico on the street, or go to The Maple Leaf and run into somebody from Tulane. Go to The Columns for free happy hour hushpuppies, or go to Rose's and sample every savory chocolate in the case. Get a free drink at Parasol's or get a free drink at Muriel's. I have nothing to do here.

❦

My first memory is falling into a sink of soapy water. There was wallpaper with faint mustard flowers.

❦

I have memorized the number of the Discover. I discover all over again the depth of its promise. Sixteen digits, an international phone number I know by heart. The more I punch those numbers, the closer I get to Boulder.

❦

It is easier to stay on a couch if you hang out all night. I hate hanging out all night, trying to pretend like I'm not down in a bag of dope.

I know every single-stall, sturdy-lock bathroom in this city. The places I can sit on the toilet and rest, let myself nod, get right if I need to.

∾

On the bathroom walls:
"Love means it's wet when he sticks his dirty fingers in it." -Ghandi
Coke's got me thinkin real clearly. I miss you baby.
"It's easy for us to say: God, forgive, God. But he didn't. He crucified him." -C.S. Lewis
Russell Batiste is a crackhead!!! And a shitty drummer!!! Suck the heads

∾

Chip sees me as a bratty thirteen-year-old, not grown into her tits yet. He no longer believes in accidents like misplacing a bag or the family discount. Family, it seems, refers to an address and not an identity. Chip thinks it is time I learned how to help myself.

∾

In the dreams:
Water
Apples
Lawyers
Judges
Sterling silver bracelets
Pomegranates
Socks
Dumpsters
Debutantes
Hoop skirts
Silverware

Water
Teeth
Apples

∾

There are kids scamming bucks off tourists in the Quarter. Kids pushing each other in strollers, kids roller skating into the Moonlight demanding free chicken fingers. Kids on the side of Claiborne selling apples. Where are these children coming from and why aren't they in school?

∾

XIV

The list of my no mores keeps getting longer.

No more going topless in the photo booth at The Saint. I've said it before and I'll probably say it again. Everyone in the 10th ward has seen my tits.

No more throwing tequila shots in the fake fern. No more stealing the quarters off dollar-and-a-quarter tips for the juke box. I'm a bartender for Christ sakes, don't I have any loyalty at all?

And no more playing White Wedding. I will definitely stop playing White Wedding.

❧

Mack says I got lice from the couch at The Saint, but I never sit on that couch, The Saint is all about up, keep working the room.

But I'll put it on the list for good measure: no more getting lice at The Saint.

❧

If you have to go home with someone, go home with someone who won't be offended by your couch requests.

∾

And no more flirting with the girls who have bangs.

No more dancing when they play Michael Jackson.

∾

No more Dirty Notes, Red-Headed Sluts, Rusty Nails, and no more Jagermeister. I said it. No more Jagermeister.

∾

I no longer pay cover charges. I've given all those bouncers free drinks at the Moonlight—five dollars to see the same horns again? I have more self-respect than that.

∾

No more using the payphone. In fact, no more phone calls at all.

∾

No more bringing the spoon and the rig to the bathroom, no more pockets full of foil.

∾

No more talking about how I'm gonna leave. That ticket is crumbly inside my purse.

If I'm gonna be here, I'm gonna be.

I'm gonna learn to sit in the place I am, without the spoon up my sleeve.

❧

No more sleeves, I'm baring my arms and showing what chicken flapping really looks like. Fuck those pretty girls in the photo booth. With their skinny arms. No one knows their names. No more trying to fuck the pretty girls in the photo booth. They're all prudes, and I'm not a lesbian.

❧

No more banging on the bathroom door from the inside. I'm never locked in. And no more coming through the back door. The cooks aren't worth the smile. No more walking around the serving side of the bar to make my own Caucasians. I'm going to learn appropriate boundaries. No more sneaking chicken fingers in my pants pockets.

❧

No more shit-talking Mack like nobody knows who he is. This is his neighborhood too. No more fake names and fake places I'm from. No more shut-your-mouth-with-a-pipe-and-make-friends moments. No more glass stem, bell ringing before the DJ starts again. No more DJs. No more tabs, no more lines, no more specials with my name on them.

No more trips, no more spills, no more talking about horns.

❧

No more talking. Lord knows I talk too much.

∾

No more laughing at my own jokes, no more seat checking. No more spending all the tips and needing a front from Ra. No more bringing Ra around here, everybody knows us. No more knowing us. No more wigs. No more sweaters—let them see the smeared make up over the train tracks on my forearms. Follow the tracks to get red. Got it? See it? Find that red.

∾

No more talking about finding red. Everyone's absolutely exhausted by me.

∾

No more double neats. No more burlesque. No more climbing on the roof in push-up bras. No more talking to men with skinny jeans, or cut-off pants, or paint-splattered cords. I will date a man who wears slacks.

No more saying I love you. That doesn't make anything better.

∾

No more leaving my cigarettes burning by the record player, no more scratching the records on purpose.

∾

No more explaining the saints, everyone here went to Catholic school anyway.

☙

No more blinking the lights like intermission's over—no one will leave until they're good and ready. No more corny dogs and no more quarter cigarettes, I'm going to buy a pack. No more two drinks at a time orders. No more extra lemon. No more finishing strangers' drinks when they go to the bathroom.

☙

No more trying to find my shoes. Whatever dumpster Mack threw them in, they're gone already.

☙

No more pretending to be deaf. No more dirty talk. And no more brushing my hand across anyone's ass.

☙

No more looking for another fix. No more fixing anything. You're not fucking broken, bitch. Stop trying to fix it all the time.

☙

No more no more no more. I'm all together done.

When I say it like that, all together, sewn into those stitches, it could be true. I could never do any of the no mores ever again. The problem is what do I do instead?

☙

XV

It's already hurricane season again. It's already been Arlene, Bret, Cindy, Dennis, Emily, Franklin, Gert, Harvey, Irene, and Jose. But it's always the same thing here. Hurry up and wait, hurry up and wait. Talk about rain, sit on the stacked highway, lose a night of tips. I know better. I know it's not the rain that kills you. The rain is just like the dope—the more it almost kills you, the more you know you'll survive it.

I still and always have to be at work. Clock in. If I scurry quick, I'll be able to make it on time.

∽

These roots pushing through the sidewalks—it's something I like about this place. We're so low to the ground, everything is an uphill climb.

Sometimes I wonder how flat my life would be if I didn't make mountains in front of my heart.

∽

Things I know I will forget:
    How the light hits the Mississippi on a drunk morning
    and makes you want to swim
    The sound of brass blown through thick air
    The way Mack smells like olives and limes and cigarette
    smoke
    Felicity to Camp
    The number to the Verdi Mart and the hangover special
    at The Saint
    How much crème de menthe goes in a grasshopper
    The way the trees bend into each other like they help
    each other to keep being trees
    How mold feels on the bottom of my toes
    Ra's hair tickling my cheek
    The smell of quinine powder
    All 16 of those Discover digits

Before I knew what dope made me feel like, I knew what New Orleans felt like, and it felt the same.

That first time I heard a horn in my hip or the way powdered sugar melts on fried dough.

I think it's a piece of ripped tire at first, stripped off in a pothole, sizzling on the street corner. But it's a bird. It's tiny, but splayed on the cement I can see how thick its feathers are, how dirty. It's all guts and maggots.

I sidestep the whole thing. I'm going to be late.

～

Trying to make a list in my head of words that rhyme with tolerance, but I turn back.

～

I pick up the mangled bird body with its maggots and its purple blood and look around for a pretty place to bury her.

Right here by the bush, I've got no idea what kind of bush it is, but there are wide pink flowers and thick branches and it feels like a good place to rest.

I try to dig a hole with a broken branch, but that's a dumb idea. I might have to give up my mission and make sure she's in the shade.

But—out of my pouch of secret, special things—a spoon.

I rub the black clean off the back and dig a hole, I could keep digging 'til I hit red clay, get out of town that way, but it'd be hit water here. The hole's about as deep as a mixing bowl and I lay her in gentle. I think I should say a few words but I'm not sure what to say. I rip out a few pages from my notebook. I find the list of dead people and lay it right over her belly.

"There," I say.

The dirt feels soft and warm. I drop the spoon in the hole and let my fingernails get grimy, pushing earth so hot it burns into my palms. I wonder how long it will be until this whole place is underwater, how long it will be until bird bones and spoons float down Felicity Street.

Acknowledgements

I'm grateful to have the opportunity to acknowledge the people who made it possible for me to write this book.

Thanks to Marc Nieson for the guidance and breakfast, and to Lori Jakiela, Sheryl St. Germain and Kate Zambreno for their encouragement and generosity.

The earliest and most supportive readers, who helped Claire find her way out: Sarah Waite Daly, Elizabeth Lark-Riley, Ashley Schor, Janet Jensen, Najeeb Sabour and Patrick DeOre. Thank you for nurturing the first drafts. I couldn't ask for a stranger or more honest art family.

Thank you, thank you, thank you to Dave Newman, who would tell me I only have to write it once. Thank you to Mike Baron and White Gorilla Press for your vision.

Special thanks to Ben and Rosalie Gwin.

This book would not have been possible without the insights and wisdom of Heinz Aeschbach, Coleen Moreno, and Heidi Van Doeren. Thank you for your difficult and necessary work in the world.

I'd be remiss not to thank my students who challenge me every day to be better and braver, especially the students at Allegheny County Jail and Sojourner House, who made this book matter more.

To Diane McQuarie and Paul Wilson, my deepest gratitude for the invaluable gift of time to finish this manuscript; and to Mildred Collins, thank you for the graceful example of how a woman makes beautiful things. To my fierce competitors in the SFO, I am lucky to walk through the red door on Mediterranean and be home.

Made in the USA
Lexington, KY
01 July 2014